Your Questions, God's Answers

PETER J. KREEFT

Your Questions, God's Answers

IGNATIUS PRESS   SAN FRANCISCO

Cover by Roxanne Mei Lum
Art by Christopher J. Pelicano

© 1994, Ignatius Press
All rights reserved
ISBN 0–89870–488–X
Library of Congress catalogue number 93–80505
Printed in the United States of America

For Gregory and Nicholas

CONTENTS

PREFACE

I originally wrote this book as an introduction to a Bible that was especially for teenagers. But the questions I asked were questions all of us ask in one way or another, at any age. I tried to present God's answers to those questions in a simple and comprehensible way. Because they are God's answers, however, they are profound as well as simple. So this book is one that I hope will be useful to anyone who has questions about God and about life.

But I am adding a special note to parents and to teenagers because I know that many of them have special need for a book like this.

To Parents

For most teenagers, religion and "real life" are two different worlds. One world—the world they live in—is full of questions; and the other world is God's answers, God's truth. This book tries to make those two worlds meet.

Why do teenagers put religion and life in separate compartments? Often, because *we* do. They learn what religion really means in life from us, not from their religion teachers. If it looks like a weak and wimpy mishmash of dull and toothless cliches to them, then we have one of two possible problems. Either that's how it looks to us too, or else we aren't getting across to them how it really looks to us.

If it's the first problem, we need a faith-lift first. You can't give what you don't have. We can't expect our kids to buy a product labelled "Do as I say, not as I do."

But if it's the second problem, maybe this book can help. I think many parents are in the second class. It's hard to talk to teenagers about deep and personal things most of the time. They fear being embarrassed more than anything else in the world. And so do we sometimes! They'll listen to wisdom better if it doesn't come wrapped in words of parental authority. They'll open the door of their minds and hearts to divine truth if only it doesn't come dressed in parent-shaped clothes. That's why I wrote this book—for you to at least leave around the house to read, or (better) to give to, or (best of all) to talk with them about. Here is God's naked truth without parental clothing (without yours, anyway). Here is what the Bible and the Church say about teenagers' deepest questions.

We're all only mail carriers. God wrote the letter. The Bible is the "Word of God" to man, not man's speculations about God. All I do in this book is a little match-making, bringing together the Word of God (which is first of all Jesus, secondarily the Bible, the book about Him) and the teenager: Michael, meet Jesus; Jesus, meet Michael. Jennifer, meet Jesus; Jesus, meet Jennifer.

To Teenagers

I assume you've read the stuff above To Parents. Good. Religion isn't about hiding anything; it's about truth. Questioning is a road to truth. All honest questions are good questions. Jesus never discouraged his disciples' questions. He gave them straight answers, even though some of the answers weren't easy to accept. I want to do the same.

This book is full of questions—the ones my own four teenagers asked, and the ones I think you ask too. I tried to give honest answers to each one, even when you might not like all the answers, because I don't think God wants any of us to sacrifice honesty at any time for anything. Not even for being liked.

The Bible's answers to your questions come in two forms. First, there are words. This Book is called "The Word of God". Second, and more completely, they come in the form of a Person, Jesus Christ. He is also called "The Word of God". The words in the Bible are like molecules of his face. It's all about him.

PETER J. KREEFT

1. How can I find out who I really am?

Young people wonder "Who am I, really?" more often than older people do. Older people often think this is because young people know so much less. I think it is because young people know something *more*—one thing, at least, that older people often forget: that everybody's real self is a mystery, that once we stop fooling ourselves, we recognize that we don't know who we really are. The whole human race can learn this one great lesson, at least, from teenagers: to be human is to wonder who you really are.

Lesson One is to know that we don't know. Socrates, the great ancient Greek philosopher and "the father of philosophy", was called the wisest man in the world by the Delphic oracle (prophet); and the only way Socrates could interpret that saying was that he was wise only because he alone knew he was *not* wise.

In other words, there are only two kinds of people in this world: the wise, who know they are fools, and fools, who think they are wise. Read more about this in Proverbs 14:33, Isaiah 29:13–14, and 1 Corinthians 1:19–20.

Jean Vanier, the founder of an international organization for helping the multiply handicapped, says that the handicapped have taught him something about himself that is more valuable than anything he has ever taught them about themselves. From them he has learned that "we are *all* 'the handicapped'."

All of us, at any age, can have an "identity crisis". To be human is to lack knowledge of our complete identity, to know only what we have been *so far*, not what we are yet to be. Day by day, year by year, choice by choice, we make ourselves into *this* kind of person or *that* kind of person. Every time we change anything in the world, we also change ourselves a little. Every time we help or harm another, we help or harm ourselves. Our selves are always under construction.

Who then can possibly know my whole self? Much of me *is* no longer; for it is in the dead past, and no one remembers it all. Much of me *is* not yet; for it is in the not-yet-born future, and no one knows what the future holds.

Except one. God, our Creator, knows us, all of us, because he designed us, just as a writer designs characters in a novel. Only our Author knows us completely. In God's mind, and there alone, can we find the secret of our identity. God alone knows all things, our past, our present, and our future.

Therefore only by finding God can I find my true self. That's where the secret of my identity *is*. To try to find out who I am by ignoring my Creator is like trying to find out who a character is by ignoring the character's author.

But how can *I* know *God*? I'm only a human being, and not the most brilliant human being in the world, by any means. How could little me possibly figure out the mind of the great God?

No way. But I *can* know God on one condition: if God takes the initiative and tells me about himself and about myself, if God teaches me, if God "reveals" himself (Jn 6:44–45).

That's what the Bible is: God's revelation, God's words about who he is and who we are.

2. How will the Bible help me to know myself?

The Bible is God's book, God's word to us. God "inspired" the human authors of this book. That means that each book in the Bible has *two* authors, the human one and the divine one. The Bible is the word of God in the words of men.

That name, "the word of God", is also the name of a person. Jesus is also called "The Word of God" (Jn 1:1, 14; Rev 19:13). The Bible, like Jesus, has two natures, human and divine.

Like Jesus, the Bible is *wholly* human and *wholly* divine at once. It's not that some parts of it are only human and other parts only divine. All of it is human, for it was written by human beings, and all of it is divine, for these human writers were all inspired by God. That does not mean that God whispered in their ears the exact words to write, but that God providentially arranged for these writers to write just what he wanted us to know. He also providentially arranged for the Church, which Jesus left us, to pick just the right books to be included in the "canon", or list of books in the Bible.

Now since the Bible is God's book, and since God holds the secret of your identity (question 1), therefore to find the secret of your identity you must read the Bible.

You get to know yourself only by getting to know God your Author. But you get to know God most perfectly by getting to know Jesus, "the visible likeness of the invisible God" (Col 1:15). Therefore you get to know yourself best only by getting to know Jesus.

He is the main point of this whole book.

3. How can I understand the Bible?

There's a right and a wrong way to read the Bible. The wrong way is to look *at* it. The right way is to look *along* it. It is like a finger, pointing beyond itself to Jesus.

An animal can only look *at* things. When you point to your cat's food with your finger, your cat will look at your finger. But a human being can also look *along* things, can treat a thing as a *sign*, can ask what it *signifies*, what it means.

What this book signifies, the whole meaning or significance of the Bible, is Jesus. Even the Old Testament points to Jesus. It was written centuries before Jesus, but it points forward to him (Lk 24:25–27). Jesus once said to the Jewish leaders of his day who studied their Scriptures (the Old Testament) but did not believe in him, "You study the Scriptures, because you think that in them you will find eternal life. And these very Scriptures speak about me! Yet you are not willing to come to me in order to have life" (Jn 5:39–40).

Imagine how foolish someone would be if they looked at all the details of a painting of someone's face and then didn't recognize the real person when that person showed up. That's what you do if you read the Bible without getting to know Jesus.

The whole Bible is a portrait of Jesus. Every part is like a line in his face. The point of reading this book is to get to know him, and the best place to begin reading about him is in the Gospels.

The four Gospels are four different accounts of the life of Jesus by four of his disciples. I suggest you read Luke's Gospel first, because it is probably the easiest and most exciting one. Then read the Acts of the Apostles, Luke's story of the early Christian Church.

Browse around in this book as you would wander around in a large and beautiful garden. There is no one method or gimmick for reading the Bible. No one can understand *everything* in it, and no one can miss getting *something* valuable out of it. It is like a friend that way. Which of your friends understands *everything* in you? Not one. But which of your friends understands *nothing* about you? Not one. This book is your friend. You can get to know it more and more every day, for it is God's revelation, and you get to know God more and more every day. One thing is certain: until you die, you will never outgrow this book.

4. Where did I come from? Where am I now? Where am I going?

If you're asking those questions, you're asking the three most important questions about life. The Bible is the most important book in the world because it answers those three questions.

Where did I come from? The Bible's first words are: "In the beginning, . . . God created heaven and earth" (Gen 1:1). And in that universe "God created human beings, making them to be like himself" (Gen 1:27). King David, who wrote many of the Psalms, on one occasion prayed to God,

> You created every part of me;
>   you put me together in my mother's womb. . . .
> When my bones were being formed,
>   carefully put together in my mother's womb,

when I was growing there in secret,
    you knew that I was there—
    you saw me before I was born.
The days allotted to me
    had all been recorded in your book,
    before any of them ever began.

(Ps 139:13, 15–16)

Where am I now? In God's universe, in God's story. History is his-story. My life is part of that story. Human stories are inside life—inside history, parts of history. But all of history, including my life, is inside God's story. In Thornton Wilder's play *Our Town*, Emily signs her school textbooks with this address:

Grovers Corners
New Hampshire
United States of America
North America
Western Hemisphere
Earth
Solar System
Milky Way Galaxy
Universe
Mind of God

Where am I going? That depends on me. God gave each of us the gift of free will, free choice. He offers us eternal life with him in Heaven. It is like a marriage proposal. We are free to say yes or no. If we say yes, then the answer to the question "Where am I going?" is: Home. And the road home is Jesus. Jesus said, "I am the way, the truth, and the life; no one goes to the Father except by me" (Jn 14:6). "God loved the world so much that he gave his only Son, so that everyone who believes in him may not die but have eternal life" (Jn 3:16).

5. What do I really want out of life?

Perhaps that is the wrong question. Perhaps you should be asking what life wants out of you.

"What do I want out of life?"—that sounds like life is a supermarket, and you *get* things out of it. "What does life want out of me?"—that sounds like life is more like a friend, and you *give* as much as you get.

If there is no God, then life is indeed like a supermarket—a large material thing that you can manipulate to your own convenience. But if God stands behind life, and in it, then you are dealing with a Person, not just a Thing. And you don't ask what you can "get out of" a person, unless you're treating a person like a thing. That's what slavery is, really—treating a person as a thing, using persons as mere means to what you want.

So let's change the question from "What do I expect from life?" to "What does life expect from me?" What are the challenges that life has given to me? Being alive means meeting challenges: growing up, making friends, relating to your family, succeeding in school, career, marriage—all these things are challenges, and we respond to them. Responsibility means response-ability, ability to respond to life's challenges. Growing up means accepting response-ability.

How does God come into this growing-up? In two ways. First, God is the only totally grown-up. (The great scientist, doctor, and musician Albert Schweitzer said when he was seventy, "I still don't know what I want to be when I grow up.") God has responsibility for the whole universe. To become more responsible, more grown-up, is to become more like God. (See Jn 13:13–17 and 2 Pet 1:3–9.)

But in the second place, God is also forever young. He never gets bored or tired, even in making millions of blades of grass, one after another—like a little child saying, "Do it again!" And he surprises you—read the Bible and you will find that surprise is one of the marks of God's presence. Stay close to God and you will stay young forever.

> He fills my life with good things
> so that I stay young and strong like an eagle.
>
> (Ps 103:5)

> Those who trust in the LORD for help
> will find their strength renewed.
> They will rise on wings like eagles;
> they will run and not get weary;
> they will walk and not grow weak.
>
> (Is 40:31)

6. I'm afraid to die.

Psychologists tell us that even young children are afraid of death. There's nothing wrong with you if you're afraid to die; maybe there's something wrong with you if you aren't!

There are two reasons why we're afraid to die. One is that death is the great unknown, and we naturally fear the unknown, like a dark room. Christianity sheds light on this darkness (Prov 14:27). Christ assures us that there is life after death by preaching it (Jn 3:36), but most of all by *showing* us the Resurrection from the dead (Mk 16:6).

The second reason we fear death is that we're afraid to meet God face-to-face because we know, all of us, deep down, that we don't deserve God or Heaven. "There's a little bad in the best of us", and the best of us are the first to admit it. "Death gets its power to hurt from sin" (1 Cor 15:56).

Would you like to meet God face-to-face right now, with no defenses, no hiding, no evasion? That's like asking whether you would like it if every thought that you have thought today, every desire and feeling that you have had today, were played on the six o'clock news for the whole world to see.

Jesus came into this world to take care of the sin problem. The essential message of Christianity is that Jesus saves us from sin. He paid the price for sin: death. In the King James Version, 1 Corinthians 15:56 reads, "The sting of death is sin", and that sting was put into Christ on the Cross. Death is now like a bee without a stinger: it can't hurt us. Death brings us into God's presence, and we have a Savior who has reconciled us to God, made peace, bought Heaven for us.

God has changed death from a monster to a mother. Instead of a monster waiting to devour us, it is a mother giving birth to us. This whole world is like a giant womb, and when we die it is like being born into the far greater world, God's world. He is waiting with arms ready to receive us.

It's O.K. if you're afraid to die. But remember Jesus'

promise, "I am the Resurrection and the Life. Whoever believes in me will live, even though he dies" (Jn 11:25).

God did not make death. When a loved one dies, do not say, "God took him." Death took him, but God took death. God tamed the monster. This was foretold in the Old Testament when Isaiah the prophet wrote, "The Sovereign LORD will destroy death forever! He will wipe away the tears from everyone's eyes" (Is 25:8). It was accomplished by Jesus' Resurrection from the dead. Because we belong to him who conquered death, Saint Paul can say, "I am certain that nothing can separate us from his love: neither death nor life . . . there is nothing in all creation that will ever be able to separate us from the love of God which is ours through Christ Jesus our Lord" (Rom 8:38–39).

7. If God loves us, why does he let us die?

We usually ask that question when a friend dies, especially when the friend is young. No one on earth knows why God allows one person to live to an old age and another to die young. But be sure of two things: God knows everything that happens and everything that is going to happen, and whatever God does or allows to happen, his motive is his love for us.

We do not know God's *timing*, why he lets an individual die at just the time he does. But we do know God's *strategy*, why he lets us die at all. Death, says the Bible, came into the world as a result of sin (Gen 3; Rom 6:23). Once the human race rebelled against God, death was the inevitable result, simply because God is the source of all life, and when you rebel against God you rebel against life.

Just imagine if there were no death. You would live here on earth forever, just as you live now. Would you prefer that? How long do you think it would take you to be bored? A hundred years? A thousand? A million? If we lived forever in our present condition, we would not be happier, but miserable. C. S. Lewis says, "We are like eggs at present. And you can't just go on being a good egg forever; you must hatch or go bad." Death is like hatching. We come out of the egg of this universe and our old body, and we are born into God's world, Heaven, and into the new body God prepares for us, our resurrection body, like Christ's.

Death is the hard way into Heaven. If we had not sinned, we would not need to die. We would have gone to Heaven as Jesus did. He never sinned and therefore did not have to die. But Jesus died anyway, freely, for us, to take the sting of death away from us.

God lets us die because he *does* love us, not because he doesn't love us. Death is like an operation, and God is like the surgeon. The poet T. S. Eliot calls Christ "the wounded surgeon". Death is our healing from all earthly ills.

8. How can I know what God wants of me?

If you really want to know, you can. Jesus promised, "Seek and you will find; . . . anyone who seeks will find" (Mt 7:7–8). If you are really asking the question "How can I know what God wants of me?" because you love him and want to please him, then you certainly *will* find out what he wants. Jesus said, "Blessed are those who hunger and thirst for righteousness, for they shall be satisfied." (Mt 5:6).

How will God let you know his will for you?

He has already done so. He has let us all know the most important things he wants from us, he has revealed his will for us, in three public ways.

First and foremost, in Jesus, God's Son, God incarnate. The Author stepped into his play as one of his characters to tell (and show) the other characters what he wants them to know and do and be.

Second, this book, the Bible, which records the words of Jesus and tells us about his work, is God's written word, God's speech to us down through the centuries.

Third, we can look to the Church, appointed by Christ to preserve and proclaim his Word to the world. Perhaps your next question is "What right does the Church have to tell me what to believe and what to do?" The answer is found on pages 28–29.

In these three ways you will find what God wants from all of us. But what about what he wants from you in particular? How can you get God's point of view on what you should do with your life, and how to make specific, difficult decisions?

The answer is very simple. He has promised that if we really want to know, we will. When people asked Jesus how they could know his teaching, he said, "If any man's will is to do his [the Father's] will, he shall know whether the teaching is from God or whether I am speaking on my own authority" (Jn 7:17). In other words, if your *will* is right, lined up with God's will, if you want to do God's will, then you will *know* it. So concentrate on getting your will and heart in line with God. The way to "discern", or clearly see, God's will for you and your life is not first cleverness but prayer, not calculation but sincerity, not figuring out but loving.

9. Isn't religion only for "religious people"?

No. *Religion* means "relationship" (with God), and that's for everybody, because everybody is God's creature and loved one.

Religion is not for people who feel religious. You don't have to feel religious at all. You can be bored in church and still not be bored with God, still believe and hope and love God. Religion is not about religion; religion is about God. True religion isn't in love with itself but with God.

And what are "religious people" anyway? The person who asks that question ("Isn't religion only for religious people?") probably thinks of religious people as wimps or sissies or squares or nerds. Was Jesus any of those things?

You don't start out by thinking, "I'm a religious person", then believe. You don't think, "I'm feeling kind of religious today. I think I'm in the market for a god. Do you have one I could worship, please?"

The five main pillars of our Catholic religion are for everybody.

1. The heart of the Catholic religion, and also of the Protestant and Jewish and Muslim religions, is this: "The LORD—and the LORD alone—is our God. Love the LORD your God with all your heart, with all your soul, and with all your strength" (Deut 6:4–5). Jesus said of that com-

mandment, "This is the greatest and the most important commandment" (Mt 22:38).

2. "The second most important commandment is like it: 'Love your neighbor as you love yourself'" (Mt 22:39).

3. The glue that sticks us to God, the "mediator" between God and humanity, the One who makes the religious relationship possible for us is Jesus, the God-man. He's for everyone, too. He said, "I am the way, the truth, and the life; no one goes to the Father except by me" (Jn 14:6).

4. The way we know Jesus is through his Church's teaching about him. Therefore, the Church is for everybody, too.

5. So is the Bible, the Church's book.

People can be religious about many things. Some people worship money, or pleasure, or power, or their job, or the State. There are no non-religious people; there are just false gods.

10. What right does the Church have to tell me what to believe and what to do?

This is a very good question, and the Bible is a good place to start in finding an answer. Read, in order, these Scriptures: John 17:20–23; 1 Timothy 3:15; 2 Corinthians 5:17; John 21:15–17; Luke 22:31–32; Matthew 16:18; John 14:9–12, 15–17, 23–24.

If the Church is only an organization of human beings, then it has no right to tell you what to believe or what to do. But if the Church is the teacher Jesus left on earth to tell us his words and his will and to continue his work on earth, then the Church has its right from Jesus, her founder. Further, Jesus has this right from his Father, for he is the Son of God. He is just as divine as his Father, just as you are just as human as your human father.

God has the right to tell us what to do because he created us and designed us (Gen 1:26–27; Rom 5:14–18). He gave us our very existence, as an author gives his characters existence. Doesn't an author have the right to tell his characters what to do?

The analogy fails here, for we have free will, as characters in a piece of fiction do not. We can choose to love and obey our Author or to rebel against him. Even when we rebel against God, God keeps loving us (Heb 12:5–11). His love is another thing that gives him the right to tell us what to do. It's for our good and out of his love that he directs us (Heb 12:9–11). He made the world and he knows what roads through life make us happy and bring us home to him, and which do not. His directions for our lives are his all-knowing and all-loving travel plan through earth to Heaven.

When the Church teaches something we find hard or don't feel like doing, for example, in the area of sexual ethics, we have to choose: Do we set ourselves up as God and judge God's ideas by our own ideas, or do we judge our ideas by God's ideas? He designed the machine; he has a right to write the operator's manual.

11. Why am I unhappy?

Saint Augustine answered that question at its root when he wrote, "You have made us for Yourself and [therefore] our hearts are restless until they rest in You."

If God has made us and designed us to be happy with him, then nothing else can take his place. God is the food our spirits need to eat. Other things will make our body happy (Eccl 2:24; 3:13; 5:18–20), but not our spirit, our soul, our true self. Other things will make us happy for a while, but not for long. Other things will make us happy on a superficial level, but not deep down.

In the Bible we read that all happiness, all joy, all beauty come from God (James 1:17). The joy of friendship, the beauty of nature, the happiness of human love were all created by God and designed to reflect his joy and beauty, to carry a little of his joy to us as air carries the light of the sun. Every joy you ever feel is a reflection of God. God is not one of the many sources of joy, for "religious people" only (whoever *they* are). God is the source of all joys that exist. Following his way is guaranteed to lead to joy; following other roads is guaranteed to lead to misery. Read Psalm 1, which summarizes that point simply but poetically. The point is made literally thousands of times in the Bible. Its lesson is really incredibly simple. Believe and love and obey God, and you will be happy.

But, you may say, the source of my unhappiness comes from problems with people here, not with God—with parents or friends or relatives or authority figures. Perhaps. But the root of the problem goes back to your relationship with God. Here is Thomas Merton's two-step diagnosis of all problems in human relationships: "We are not at peace with others because we are not at peace with ourselves. And we are not at peace with ourselves because we are not at peace with God." Adam and Eve certainly learned that lesson when they disobeyed God. Read Genesis 3.

Do you want to be happy? Then give God a chance. He is stronger than any human need, any unhappiness, even any sin. "Where sin increased, God's grace increased much more" (Rom 5:20).

The great American poet T. S. Eliot said that the greatest line in all the world's literature is the simple line from Dante, perhaps the greatest poet of all time: "In his will, our peace."

Try it. You'll like it.

12. What shall I do with my life?

"God has made us what we are, and in our union with Christ Jesus he has created us for a life of good deeds, which he has already prepared for us to do" (Eph 2:10).

The age of youth, especially the teenage years, is like setting sail out of a safe, small harbor (your home and family). Once the ship is at sea, it can turn many different ways and set its course for many different destinations. Soon, you will be making decisions that will affect the rest of your life: college, friends, marriage, career. You may be feeling insecure, unsure and afraid, like a small boat sailing out into a great, dark, stormy sea.

There is One greater than the sea, One who stilled the storms. Read Luke 8:22-25. If you "put your hand in the hand of the Man who stilled the waters", he will lead you. He promised, "I will be with you always" (Mt

28:20, the very last verse in that Gospel). If you trust him to lead you, then your path through life will be the right one because it will be his path.

I cannot tell you the answer to your question "What shall I do with my life?" because it is your life, not mine. But it is also God's life (Gal 2:20). He created you. He designed you. Let him design your life.

I cannot tell you the answer to your question, "What shall I do with my life?" because I do not know you personally. But he does. He knows every tiny thing about you. "Even the hairs of your head have all been counted" (Lk 12:7).

Pray for *his* guidance and you will get it. "Anyone who seeks [me] will find [me]" (Mt 7:8). He promised that, and he wants us to claim that promise.

13. What is the secret of success? I seem like a failure.

Life holds only one failure, finally: not to be God's friend.

People expect many things of us, and no one has ever lived up to everyone's expectations. Especially as a teenager: everyone expects you to do everything right, it seems. But every person who has ever lived has been a failure by someone's standards. Parents expect one thing, friends another, girlfriends one thing, boyfriends another. We are expected to succeed at home, in school, in athletics, in work, in friendship, in competition. Modern life is very competitive, and makes many people anxious about "succeeding" versus "failing". We are sometimes made to feel that we are worthwhile only if we perform well, if we succeed in coming up to others' expectations. Sometimes we even feel that we are *loved* only if we "succeed".

Jesus never treated his friends like that. In fact, he deliberately sought out the "failures" in other people's eyes, and they sought him out. Often, failures in the eyes of the world were successes in his eyes. And the reverse was also true; successes in the eyes of the world were often failures in his eyes.

Every psychology, philosophy, or social system in the world holds up an ideal for success, but Christ alone has a place for failures. Read Jesus' "Beatitudes" (Mt 5:1–14). Each one of them tells of some apparent failure, like poverty or mourning, or something silly in the eyes of the world, like humility or purity; and Jesus pronounces these blessed, successful, happy.

The explanation for these surprising, even outrageous, statements of Jesus is that *God's love* is surprising and outrageous. *He loves the unlovable.* He loves us not for what we do, not because we have succeeded in performing. We haven't. None of us has scored a passing grade on God's exam. "If we say we have no sin, we deceive ourselves, and there is no truth in us" (1 Jn 1:8).

Christianity is not competitive because Christianity is Christ and Christ is God and God is love and love is not competitive.

You are a success—an eternal success, a success forever in Heaven and a success right now in the eyes of God—if only you love God and your neighbor. True success is measured by God, not by the world, because God, not the world, is our Author and Designer, the One who determines the true values in life.

God's prescription for success is very simple. Read Psalm 1.

Here, in specific detail, is God's path to success:

1. First, God is love (1 Jn 4:8).

2. God showed his love for us by sending his Son to die for us. "God has shown us how much he loves us —it was while we were still sinners that Christ died for us!" (Rom 5:8).

3. Once we realize how much God loves us, we naturally respond by loving him. "We love because God first loved us" (1 Jn 4:19).

4. And once we realize that this is enough to make us successes in God's eyes, once we realize that all he wants from us is our love, then we are freed from anxiety about other things. Then all the other things in life can be extras, not absolute necessities.

5. And once we realize that, we probably will succeed more at them because we are no longer addicted to them, we no longer absolutely *have* to succeed at them. Fear and worry and anxiety are gone.

14. Nobody really understands me, really loves me.

It may surprise you to learn that a very large number of young people (and not only young people) feel this way, though they usually cover it up. And not all of the ones who feel unloved and misunderstood come from families broken by obvious problems like divorce, alcoholism, unfaithfulness, or physical abuse. The feeling is common in all kinds of people.

Even we as believers sometimes forget that we do have Someone who understands. If we believe that the Bible is God's Word, then we know that the most important Person of all understands us completely and loves us infinitely. (See Ps 107:1, 8, 15, 21, 31; Rom 5:8; 1 Jn 3:1; 4:19.)

Each of us has a need to be loved just for what we are, and to be understood just as we are. What we get from people is some love, not none and not an infinite amount; and some understanding, always somewhere between none at all and total understanding. No one, not even sincerely loving parents who try to understand, can understand *everything* in you. *You* don't even understand everything in you.

But God does.

All persons who ever walked this earth have had a need to be totally understood and loved at the very center of their being. And that is a need only God can fill. (See Ps 139:1–6.)

Here is God's solemn promise: "I will never leave you; I will never abandon you" (Heb 13:5). Believe that and you will know what being loved is.

But people can be God's instruments. Once you know his love, you are freed to appreciate the partial but real human loves, the never-enough but nevertheless-precious attempts of people who do care about you. Once you stop looking for divine love from human beings, once you stop placing divine hopes on human shoulders, you are freed from the disappointment that always comes from that false hope. No human being can be God to you. But he or she can be a good friend to you.

One day you may find one person who loves you more fully than anyone else, who wants to promise to love you and live with you and be faithful to you forever: the person you marry. You will choose to give your whole life, your all, to that person. Please, for the sake of your own happiness, do not even *think* of marrying anyone who loves you less than that or whom you love less than that. The love between husband and wife is tiny compared with God's love, but it is great compared with all the other loves in the world.

15. How can I stop hurting people with my words?

A hot temper and quick tongue are very hard to control. "Man is able to tame and has tamed all other creatures —wild animals and birds, reptiles and fish. But no one has ever been able to tame the tongue" (James 3:7–8).

God is the tongue-tamer. You can't do it without him. But he won't do it without you. You have already taken the first step if you—really caring—asked the question, "How can I stop hurting people with my words?" God knows that, and he is eager to help. But he wants to teach *you* self-control, so he won't do it *for* you, only *with* you. The same is true of all good things: we can't do them without God, and God won't do them without us. (Read Eph 4:29–32.)

It might help to remember that the other person, who is about to be hurt by our unloving word, stands in Jesus' place: "I tell you, whenever you did this for one of the least important of these brothers of mine, you did it for me!" (Mt 25:40).

16. I just don't get anything out of going to Mass.

Before talking about the Mass, let's see what the Bible has to say about the worship of God.

You can't understand worship unless you see it in the context of the relationship between God and his people. That relationship was like marriage. It was called the "covenant". The covenant he made with them was a relationship of love. But God did more. He also gave them a way to *see* the relationship in the worship God gave them. (The instructions for that worship are found in the books of Exodus, Leviticus, and Deuteronomy.) Their worship, with its sacrifices, was a physical expression of the relationship.

But all of that was just a shadow of the real thing (Heb 10:1), like having a picture of a turkey for Thanksgiving instead of a real turkey. Christ established a new covenant relationship when he offered himself as the true sacrifice (Heb 9:1–10:25). Christ did all that the Old Testament ritual only hinted at. His is the perfect sacrifice, his the perfect worship, and the relationship of love he established with us the perfect relationship. You have come "to Jesus, the mediator of a new covenant, and to the sprinkled blood that speaks more graciously than the blood of Abel" (Heb 12:24). This is the worship which the Catholic Mass expresses.

So what about the Mass? First, you don't go to Mass to *get* something but to *give* something: the worship of God that God deserves. At Mass the Church does something: offers the sacrifice of Jesus Christ to God the Father for the salvation of the world. The Mass is the representation of the most important event in the history of the world: the sacrificial death of Jesus for the salvation of the human race.

Second, we do it not because we feel like it but in obedience to Jesus' command. When he instituted the Mass, he commanded his disciples to "do this in memory of me" (Lk 22:19). His Church today only echoes *his* command.

Third, we *do* get something out of it: Jesus himself. "This is my body", he said. The Catholic Church has always taught that Jesus is really, truly present in the consecrated bread and wine. At Mass we "get" what we need more than anything else in the world: Jesus.

"But I don't feel anything", you may say. So what? You may not feel anything when you eat bread or take vitamins either. But they really nourish you. "For our life is a matter of faith, not of sight" (2 Cor 5:7). We believe vitamins help us because doctors tell us so. If we believe our human doctors, why not believe the divine doctor of our souls?

Our faith is not dependent on our feeling, but on the facts God has revealed to us, the truths God has assured us of. Our feelings will come, in their time, but only if we don't worry about them, only if we keep our eyes on the truth.

Faith, Fact, and Feeling walked along a wall. Fact went first, then Faith, then Feeling. But when Faith turned around to see how Feeling was doing, and took his eyes off Fact, both Faith and Feeling fell off the wall, while Fact walked on alone.

17. How can I stop following the crowd?

The answer to this question is related to the answer to question 12, "What shall I do with my life?" Question 12 is about knowing something: God's will. This question is about feeling something: being pulled away from God's will.

This time in your life is a time for gradually testing your wings, being yourself, finding out who you are. You used to be told by your parents everything you needed to know; now you have to find out more and more for yourself. It's hard to do that. The easy way out is to let the crowd do for you what your parents used to do. That's why you feel two pulls at the same time that seem opposites: the pull to be yourself as an individual, and the pull to conform to the crowd.

How can you be yourself and stop blindly following the crowd? God will free you to be yourself the more you follow him. Following God is not blind conformity, because he alone knows you perfectly: what you were, what you are, and what you will be. What God wants is for you to grow up and choose freely. He wants you to choose the *good*, and not the evil, but he wants *you* to choose. If you follow God, you will become a real individual and you won't need to blindly follow the crowd when you don't want to or don't think the crowd is right. God said, "Do not follow the majority when they do wrong or when they give testimony that perverts justice" (Ex 23:2).

We follow the crowd because we want to be accepted and liked and admired. But the people we most want to be admired by will *not* admire us for having no spine or guts. They will admire us for being courageous and strong and standing up for our beliefs. The surest way *not* to be liked is to worry a lot about being liked. The surest way to be accepted is just to be yourself and not worry about being accepted. Then when you *are* accepted, you will know that it is for being what you really are, not for faking it and compromising for the sake of being accepted (Prov 21:21). Read Joshua 24:14–15.

God is like salt: he brings out the special flavor in every different food. Salt makes steak steakier, and fish fishier, and eggs eggier. So God frees you to be more yourself, not less (Jn 8:32). The way to get a real personality, a real self, is from the Creator and Designer and Lover of selves, not from the crowd.

Jesus said to his disciples (us!), "You are like salt for all mankind. But if salt loses its saltiness, there is no way to make it salty again. It has become worthless, so it is thrown out and people trample on it" (Mt 5:13). The way to be trampled on is to become a nobody. The way to enliven and help others is to be a somebody. And the way to be a somebody is to love and follow the One who makes you somebody, not the ones who make you nobody.

There are only three reasons for ever doing anything, and "everyone's doing it" is not one of them: (1) because you *ought* to (a moral duty), (2) because you *have* to (a practical necessity, like eating), or (3) because you, you yourself, really *want* to.

For further reading, see Psalm 1.

18. What are television and movies teaching me?

Jesus told stories most of the time, and these stories powerfully put across his set of values to people. Some examples of Jesus' parables, or stories, are found in Matthew 18:21-25; Mark 4:1-9, 13-19; Luke 10:25-37; and 14:15-21. The values Jesus taught are the true values, because he is the Teacher of Truth.

But television and movies also teach us values. They don't just entertain us; they also teach us. There is a set of values in every story. Sometimes their values are obvious; sometimes they are hidden. The wise person is the one who looks for the values being taught and compares them with the values Jesus taught. How do you think they compare?

This does not mean you should not watch television and movies. However, it does mean you should be discriminating about what you watch—about what values you choose to make part of your life. There are many excellent television shows, and many perfectly innocent ones; there are some good, even great movies. But most of them today assume a set of values that is radically opposed to the teachings of Christ. We need to judge what we watch, say, think, and do by the standards Jesus set.

According to a recent poll, media personnel are more hostile to religion and religious values than almost any other group of people in our society. Nine out of ten never go to church. The majority say they do not even believe in the Biblical God. Because of this, most movies and television shows assume a moral code that is purely subjective (what is right is whatever you feel it is) and relative (no moral absolutes, nothing is absolutely right or wrong).

This is most obvious in the area of sex. Twenty years ago, even "sexy" movies assumed and implicitly taught the sexual morality that Christianity shares in common with many other religions and societies in history: that sex is sacred and adultery is wrong. Now, the vast majority of movies and television shows assume the opposite.

It's not just a question of what you see, how much flesh is shown. Nudity is not necessarily sinful. It's not even just a question of lust. That's always been around, and always will be. The new thing is the justification and glorification of sex for its own sake. Sex outside of marriage is a sin because it breaks down marriage and thus the family, the basic unit of society and the basic teacher of values. Because media writers have cheapened marriage by cheapening sexual fidelity, they are at least partly to blame for much of the tragedy of divorce.

We are not living in a Christian culture. Like the early Christians, we are living in a secular and often anti-Christian culture. (Read Jesus' prayer for his disciples in John 17:6–26.) While we must not shrink away from secular culture like a turtle hiding in its shell, we must not be naïve. Take what the secular media teach you with a grain of salt, because you are, according to Jesus himself, "salt for all mankind" (Mt 5:13). Establish within yourself the true values, Christian values. The Gospel of Matthew is one of the best for learning the values Jesus taught. The Book of Proverbs contains much practical wisdom reflecting the right set of values. Also, read Paul's first letter to the Corinthians to see how he advised the

Corinthian Christians to live in the context of their very secular society.

19. How can I know whom to marry?

God has promised to guide you in all the decisions and needs of your life (Phil 4:19; Mt 7:7–11). He guided Isaac in finding a wife. (Read Genesis 24. It is a beautiful story.) He will guide you in finding a wife or husband, too, or in deciding whether to marry or not. There are three honorable states: marriage, the single life, and the priesthood or religious life. God will guide your choice —if you ask him.

"Marriages are made in Heaven." God has a perfect plan for your life and that includes a plan for your marriage. It may not seem perfect to us because it includes our mistakes and sufferings. But these too teach us and mature us. God has not promised us a rose garden. Marriage is a tough job, not a bed of roses. Or rather, it *is* a rose garden—it has the most beautiful flowers in it—but it is also full of thorns. The roses are certainly worth the thorns. But thorns—difficulties, problems—are there. Marriage is for grown-ups, for people with determination, people who are determined to *work* at it.

The three most important decisions of your life are: (1) what God to believe in (everyone, even an atheist, believes in something); (2) whether to marry and whom to marry; and (3) what career, what work, to go into. In one sense, the second is the most crucial because it is the only one that cannot be reversed. Marriage is for life. If you believe what the Church teaches—what Christ taught—

that God does not allow divorce (Mt 5:31–32, for example), then you have a wonderful security: *no matter what*, the two of you will always be married; no *thought*, even, of divorce. That awful door will never open because for a Catholic it does not *exist*.

When a man and a woman agree to let Christ be the Lord of their life together, their marriage is guaranteed by Christ himself. Please do not even *think* of marrying someone who does not believe and love the Lord. If you do, there will be *four* lords and masters competing in your marriage: you, your Lord, your partner, and his or her lord. If there is only one conductor, then the musicians play in harmony.

So the answer to the question "How can I know whom to marry?" is: (1) Ask and trust God for guidance; (2) believe and obey Christ's teachings about marriage (Mt 19:1–12; Mk 10:1–12); (3) marry only a Christian (1 Cor 7:39); and *then* (4) follow your heart. For if you are in God's will and law, God will guide you through your own heart and feelings too (Ps 37:4).

20. What is it to be a Christian?

Different people will give different answers to that question. Who has the right answer? How about Christ? Doesn't *he* have the right to answer the question what it is to be a Christian, to be his follower?

What does he say? He says his followers are to become parts of him, incorporated into his body. "I am the vine, and you are the branches" (Jn 15:5)—the same life, the same plant. A Christian is a branch of Christ, a part of Christ. Together, Christians are the Church, the body of Christ (Eph 5:30; Col 1:18). Vatican II defined the Church as "the people of God".

To be a Christian is to be part of the Church. But the Church is not just a building or just a visible institution. The visible institution is what the body looks like, its skin. But the life of the body is Christ. He is its heart, its soul.

We become a part of Christ, incorporated into Christ's body, by baptism, and we ratify that later by faith. This is described as a new birth. Nicodemus discussed this issue with Jesus (Jn 3:1–17; see also Titus 3:5). When we are baptized and believe, a new kind of life enters our soul from God. It is not biological life, the life we got from our parents, but spiritual life, supernatural life from our Father in Heaven.

So being a Christian is something more than just believing Christ's teachings and trying to obey Christ's commands. It is more than just *believing* something and *doing* something, though it is certainly those two things, too; it is *being* something, something new. "Therefore, if any one is in Christ, he is a new creation; the old has passed away, behold, the new has come" (2 Cor 5:17).

Being a Christian is like being a butterfly instead of a caterpillar. It is a real change, a change in what we *are*, not only a change in thoughts and actions, though it must include those two things, too.

Jesus used different words for this supernatural life which makes us something new. He called it "eternal life", "the kingdom of God", and the "kingdom of Heaven". He said it is the most precious and important thing in all the world, so important that it is worth giving up the whole world for it. He said, "The kingdom of Heaven is like this. A man is looking for fine pearls, and when he finds one that is unusually fine, he goes and sells everything he has, and buys that pearl" (Mt 13:45–46).

This one pearl is eternal life. It begins now, in this life, and goes to Heaven when we die. If we have this life in us from God, then we can live with God and see him and love him and enjoy him forever in an ecstasy of infinite and unthinkable bliss. If we do not have it, we are failures in the only way that really counts: eternal failures.

And all we have to do to get eternal life is to accept it in faith. It is a gift. "Come, whoever is thirsty; accept the water of [eternal] life as a gift, whoever wants it" (Rev 22:17). A gift must be freely given and freely accepted. God freely gives us this gift; we must freely accept it. We got biological life unfreely from our parents. We were not asked whether we wanted to be born. But God asks us whether we want to be born into his family. Faith means saying yes to his offer.

21. Can a Catholic be a "born-again Christian"?

To answer that, we must know what a "born-again Christian" is. Whom do we ask? How about Christ himself? He talked about being born again in John 3 (one of the very best chapters in the Bible to read and know).

What did he say? That we *must* be born again to enter his kingdom. So "born-again Christian" means simply "Christian". It's like "pizza pie". "Pizza" *means* "pie" in Italian, so "pizza pie" means "pie pie". It's a redundancy, a repetition. So is "born-again Christian". To be a Christian *is* to be born again.

But what is it to be born again? Again, whom do we ask? Let's not ask the media; let's ask Christ. The media may picture "born-again Christians" as pushy, emotional, narrow-minded, preachy, and fanatical. Sometimes people who label themselves "born-again Christians" are like that, sometimes not. But what does Christ say? He says (1) that you have to be born again to enter God's kingdom (Jn 3:3: "I am telling you the truth: no one can see the Kingdom of God unless he is born again.") and (2) that this means "born of water and the Spirit" (v. 5). "Water" refers to baptism and "the Spirit" is God the Holy Spirit. He really comes to live in our souls. This is that supernatural life we spoke of in the last question.

Catholics are Christians, and Christians are all born again, so not only *can* a Catholic be a born-again Christian, but a Catholic *must* be a born-again Christian, in the sense Jesus taught.

22. How can I be sure God loves me?

The Bible deals with that question from beginning to end. It doesn't try to prove that God exists; it shows us how God loves us. That's a more important question, because if God existed but didn't love us, we'd be in a terrible fix. If your parents didn't love you, think how terrible that would be. But it would be even more terrible if our Creator didn't love us.

How can we be sure God loves us?

First, because the Bible tells us so. It is the story of God's love for his people from the beginning. (Read Psalm 136, a song about part of that story.)

Second, because Jesus shows it, especially by dying for us. "God loved the world so much that he gave his only Son" (Jn 3:16).

Third, we can see God's love in our lives. Think of all the good things you have; "count your blessings." They all come from God: life, health, friends, food, water, sunlight, beauty, a mind, pleasure, animals, games, sleep, parents—whom can we thank for all these things? Gratitude must be a terrible feeling for an atheist. He has no God to thank.

Fourth, God must love you: he arranged to have you born. Do you realize how carefully he had to arrange that? If your parents had never met, they would not have married and you would not have been born. If your grandparents . . . it goes back to the beginning. God foresaw you when he created the first atom (Eph 1:4–5).

Fifth, if God is good, he must be loving, because love is the most important part of goodness. All the other parts—honesty and courage and justice and faithfulness —are what love is: love is courageous, love is just, and so on.

Sixth, we can know God's love for us when we pray, when we open our heart to him, and instead of *telling* him things, just *listen* to him, feel his presence. Sometimes he just makes us know he loves us, in a subtle and mysterious way. Even when we don't feel it, we can believe it is true. Remember Faith, Fact, and Feeling (question 16).

For more about God's love, read Psalm 103; Romans 5:8; 8:28–39; Titus 3:4–5 and 1 John 4:7–21.

23. If God loves me so much, why do bad things happen to me?

A man named Job asked the same question after suffering total disaster—he lost all his children and property and got a terrible disease. Three of his best friends offered explanations that seemed much too simple for Job. You can read their famous dialogue in chapters 3 through 37 in the Book of Job. Read the Lord's unsettling response to one of life's toughest questions (Job 38:1–42:6).

But the Bible has even more to say about sin and evil. There really is such a thing. This may be an unpopular teaching of Christianity, but it is also one of the most realistic. Read what the Bible has to say about the reality of evil and its impact on the world: Psalm 51:1–17; 1 Corinthians 15:21–22; Galatians 5:19–26.

Bad things happen to us not because God does not love us but because of all the evil in the world; and *that* came from human sin, not from God (Gen 3). Consider the following points:

1. To deal with evil, God sent his own Son Jesus into the middle of the worst evil in the world, crucifixion. Suffering comes with being a Christian—it's normal for the Christian (Heb 11:32–12:11; 1 Pet 4:12–16). Like a training exercise that makes our bodies strong, suffering helps to make our faith and character strong.

2. Suffering is temporary, even if it lasts a lifetime on earth. Sometimes you see a light at the end of the tunnel only to find out that it's part of a fast-approaching freight train. But don't worry. You will eventually get to the end of the tunnel. (Read Rom 8:18–23, 35–39; 1 Pet 5:8–11.)

3. God can produce good things out of bad situations (Rom 5:3–5; James 1:2–4). He has an amazing ability to transform the results of a bad situation, because although he allows evil, he also rules over it.

Saint Philip Neri said, "The cross is the gift God gives to his friends." When we suffer, we help Jesus carry his Cross. We share in his work. Saint Paul said in Colossians 1:24: "Now I rejoice in my sufferings for your sake, and in my flesh I complete what is lacking in Christ's afflictions for the sake of his body, that is, the church." This is a great mystery, and a wonderful one. It makes even suffering meaningful and full of hope.

24. Can't you be a good person without believing in Christianity?

The reason for believing in Christianity is not that it is a means to the end of making you "a good person". The reason for believing in Christianity is that it is true.

Yes, you can be a good person without believing in Christianity. Many non-Christians are very good people. But God wants us to be something more than just "good people". He wants us to share his own life and joy. Being just "a good person", compared to being what

God has designed us to be, is like being a flea compared to being a horse.

Why would you ask this question? Is it perhaps that you suspect Christianity may be true but you don't want to believe it? If so, watch out. That isn't quite honest, is it?

If it *is* true—if God does exist, and did create us, and loves us, and sent his Son Jesus to save us from sin, and wants to take us to Heaven to live with him in unimaginable happiness forever—if all this is true, then it is the most colossal truth we have ever heard. We can't use this as a mere means to the end of "being a 'good person'". That would be like using the world's greatest work of art as a paperweight.

If Christianity is true, we must believe it because it is true. If it is *not* true, we must *not* believe it, even if it does make us better people. Believing in Santa Claus might make you a better person, too, but you don't believe in Santa Claus, do you? You can't manipulate truth for the sake of anything else. Truth is an absolute.

25. What do you have to do to get to Heaven?

That is the most important question in the world. Yet most people do not know the answer to it!

Amazingly, even most Catholics do not know the answer to it, the answer the Catholic Church teaches, which is the same answer the Bible teaches, and the same answer Jesus teaches. I have taught at Catholic colleges for thirty years, and I often ask my students this simple question. Usually, only a few can give me the correct answer. I never cease to be astounded and angry at this fact. It is like going to school for fifteen years and not being able to count to ten.

Here are the answers I get most often:

1. I think if you "lead a good life", you go to Heaven.

2. If you're "basically a good person", you go to Heaven.

3. If you "just do your best", God accepts you.

4. If you're sincere, God accepts you.

5. If you try.

6. Good people go to Heaven; evil people go to Hell.

7. Only Catholics go to Heaven.

The trouble with all seven of these answers is, of course, that they are our guesses. Wouldn't it be sensible to find out instead what *God* says about it? Now that we're finished playing the silliest of all games, playing God, will the real God please stand up?

He has done so; he has revealed to us the way to Heaven. The way is very simple. It is only "one way". The way is Jesus, the man who said "I am the way" (Jn 14:6).

Jesus, the Church Jesus founded, and the Church's book, the Bible, all say the same thing, in many ways, many times.

The Bible is very clear: " 'What must I do to be saved?' . . . 'Believe in the Lord Jesus, and you will be saved' " (Acts 16:30–31). "God loved the world so much that he gave his only Son, so that everyone who believes in him may not die but have eternal life" (Jn 3:16).

This belief always means two other things, too: hope and love. Faith is like the roots of the plant of our eternal life. Hope is like the stem. Love is like the flower. Christ is the life-giving ground in which the plant is rooted (Col 2:6–7). If we believe in him, we will believe in his promises, too, and that is hope. And if we believe in him, we will want to obey his law, which is to love God and our neighbor. Faith always flowers in love. "Faith without actions is dead" (James 2:26).

Faith, hope, and love are like the three legs of a single tripod, supporting the whole Christian life. "These three remain: faith, hope, and love; and the greatest of these is love" (1 Cor 13:13).

Love is the greatest thing, but we need to know where it comes from. Love comes from God, who *is* love (1 Jn 4:8). We cannot have *this* love, God-love, total love, without faith, for faith plants our souls into God.

The trouble with the seven human guesses above is that they assume (1) that you have to *do* something to get into Heaven, that you can "buy your way in" and (2) that there is some arbitrary cutoff point at which you pass God's exam. This forgets that God is not an exam-giver but a life-giver, a lover. He is more concerned with what we *are* than with what we do. He is concerned with what we *do* mainly because what we *do* helps to make us what we *are*. God wants us to become loving persons, which are the only kind of persons who will be able to *enjoy* Heaven, because that's what we do in Heaven: forget ourselves and love God and each other.

None of us can buy our way into Heaven. None of us is good enough (Is 64:6; Rom 3:23). None of us does our best. Heaven is God's free gift. It is "grace". That's why there's no cutoff point: it's a gift, not an exam. You either accept it or not.

This gift of eternal life was given to you in Baptism years ago without your free choice. Now that you are responsible for making your own decisions, you must freely choose for yourself: either to believe in Jesus Christ as the one he claims to be, your Lord and your Savior, or not. The choice is yours. You can do it right now, this very moment. It is the most important choice you will ever make.

26. How can I have my sins forgiven?

The Bible is very clear on this: "If we say that we have no sin, we deceive ourselves, and there is no truth in us. But if we confess our sins to God, he will keep his promise and do what is right: he will forgive us our sins and purify us from all our wrongdoing" (1 Jn 1:8–9).

Jesus forgives our sins. One of the things he did while he was here on earth was to forgive sins—all sins. He showed that he had the authority to forgive sins by performing miracles of healing that only God could do. (Read Mark 2:1–12.)

Only God has the authority to forgive all sins, because he is the only one against whom all sins are committed. I can forgive you for your sins against me, but I have no right to forgive you for your sins against anyone else. No human being has the right to forgive all sins; only God has that right. But Jesus constantly did just that: he forgave all sins. Those who heard him do that clearly understood that this was a claim to be God: "How does he dare talk like this? This is blasphemy! God is the only one who can forgive sins!" (Mk 2:7). They realized that Jesus had to be either God, as he claimed to be, or a very bad man, a man who blasphemed, by pretending to be God. That would make Jesus the greatest liar and fake in history.

Jesus said to his apostles, "If you forgive people's sins, they are forgiven; if you do not forgive them, they are not forgiven" (Jn 20:23). This is why the Roman Catholic Church still has the Sacrament of Reconciliation, or Penance, or Confession: in obedience to Christ.

We confess our sins to God. The priest in the confessional is only God's *representative*. But he is *God's* representative.

The Sacrament of Penance was given for forgiveness. This sacrament is not an additional burden for Catholics but an extra assurance and guarantee; not a hindrance but a help, to lighten our load, not to weigh us down. We should never be afraid to go to confession. The only one who is right to be afraid of what happens in confession is the Devil. For very great graces and help and strength are given to our souls there.

Forgiveness is not a legal deal, like a bank loan. It is the healing of a relationship. Sin means first of all breaking a relationship with God, not first of all breaking a legal deal. It is the relationship of love and trust and obedience, the relationship of "yes". Sin is saying no to God. Forgiveness is restoring the yes relationship.

27. Is *every* sin forgivable?

Perhaps you are asking that question because there is some sin you have committed, hidden or open, that you think perhaps even God cannot forgive or will not forgive. Perhaps you are afraid that God's justice is greater than God's love.

Jesus made it crystal clear that God forgives sins— all sins—if only we repent, confess our sins, and turn to God in faith for his forgiveness. Jesus told many parables about forgiveness. The most famous is the parable of the lost son in Luke 15:11–32. Here is how Jesus described the attitude of the father (God) to the runaway son who repents and comes back home to God: "He got up and started back to his father. He was still a long way from home when his father saw him. His heart was filled with pity, and he ran, threw his arms around his son, and kissed him" (Lk 15:20). God is much more eager and ready to forgive us than we are to ask for forgiveness.

God forgives *all* our sins (Col 2:13). He even forgives sins that we repeat time and time again. "Peter came to Jesus and asked, 'Lord, if my brother keeps on sinning against me, how many times do I have to forgive him? Seven times?' 'No, not seven times', answered Jesus, 'but seventy times seven'" (Mt 18:21–22). Peter thought seven times was generous, but God is more generous still. By saying seventy times seven Jesus was saying that forgiveness is to be given as often as asked for, not just 490 times.

There seems to be one "catch" to receiving God's forgiveness. However, it is not really a "catch" at all, but a necessity. It is that we must be willing to forgive others, or else we cannot be forgiven. Jesus made that clear when he told us to pray, in "the Lord's Prayer", "Forgive us the wrongs we have done, as we forgive the wrongs that others have done to us"(Mt 6:12), and immediately went on to explain, "If you forgive others the wrongs they have done to you, your Father in Heaven will also forgive you. But if you do not forgive others, then your Father will not forgive the wrongs you have done" (Mt 6:14–15).

It's not like a deal, where God says he will forgive us only if we do something in return. Rather, it's a necessity: if our hands are not open, we cannot receive a gift, and forgiveness is a free gift from God. But if our hands *are* open (so to speak) then we give as well as receive. Forgiveness is a free gift: it must be freely given and freely received, and freely passed on. If it is received but not passed on, it goes stale, like stagnant water. Look at a map of Israel. The Jordan River's waters flow *through* the Sea of Galilee, and that is why that sea is full of fish and life and fresh water. The same river flows into the Dead Sea, which has no outlet. That is why the Dead Sea lives up to its name. We must be like the Sea of Galilee, not like the Dead Sea; when we receive the waters of God's love and forgiveness, we must pass them on in order to keep them alive.

Perhaps you are asking the question "Is every sin forgivable?" with a different motive: not because of a past sin but because of a future sin. Perhaps you are planning to commit some sin and wonder whether God will forgive it. It doesn't work like that. God forgives sins only if they are sincerely repented of. If you are planning to commit a sin, you cannot at the same time be repenting of it. You cannot be both running away from God and running back to him at the same time. Sin and repentance of sin are like fire and water; they are opposites that put each other out. You must choose one or the other.

(Also read Ps 86:5; Sir 28:2; Mt 18:22–35; Heb 4:14–16; and 1 Jn 1:9.)

28. Does God love me less when I sin?

No. God loves you infinitely at all times. But you make it harder for yourself to believe in God's love and to receive it and to benefit by it each time you sin.

Nothing can stop God's love from going out from him. But you can stop it from entering into you. It is like the sunlight: nothing can stop it from coming out of the sun, because that is what the sun is made of. But you can shut your eyes or pull the shades down. God is like a million burning suns of love; nothing can stop him from loving you, any more than you can stop the sun from shining. But you can turn your back on it and run into your own shadow.

God's love is not dependent on how good we are. Jesus made that clear in a number of his parables. The shepherd (God) spent his time and effort going out to look for the one lost sheep, even though he had ninety-nine others at home that did not wander off (Lk 15:1–7). The lost son's father was looking down the road for his lost son to return and went out to meet him (Lk 15:20).

That's the kind of love we get from God: "God is love and he who abides in love abides in God, and God abides in him" (1 Jn 4:16).

When we really realize this, when it really hits home that God loves us even when we sin; when we realize that God loves us not for performing well but for being ourselves; when we realize that what God wants from us is simply our hearts; when we realize that God is a lover, not a slave master—then we naturally respond to this God with love, not with fear. "There is no fear in love; perfect love drives out all fear" (1 Jn 4:18). And love is a stronger and more effective motive than fear in avoiding sin. We don't *want* to sin against love. We feel worse about sinning against a divine Lover than against a divine slave driver.

For more about God's love, read Psalm 51; John 15: 12–17; Ephesians 2:4–5; and 2 Thessalonians 2:16–17.

29. Is avoiding sin the most important thing?

No. First of all, avoiding evil is only a means to the greater end of doing good and being good. Of course, we cannot do good or be good *unless* we avoid evil and obey the Commandments, but we should think much more about good than about evil: "Fill your minds with those things that are good and that deserve praise: things that are true, noble, right, pure, lovely, and honorable" (Phil 4:8).

Second, even moral goodness, even obeying the Ten Commandments, is not the most important thing there is. God and your neighbor are even more important (Mk 12:28–31). But once again, unless we obey the Commandments, we can't truly honor God and love our neighbor. The commandments are means, ways to love God and neighbor.

When God led his chosen people out of the slavery of Egypt (which is like sin) into the Promised Land (which is like Heaven) through the desert (which is like life), he led them past Mount Sinai, where they received the Ten Commandments. They did not stop at Sinai. It was a way station. The Ten Commandments were their marching orders. Their destination was Yonder.

Thinking about sin too much produces worry and fear. Thinking about sin too little produces indifference. Sin is like disease. You can think too much or too little about it. If you think too much about disease, you will worry yourself sick, literally. That is what a "hypochondriac" does. If you think too little about it, you can risk your health and fall into disease.

We should make a short, regular "examination of conscience", perhaps once a day, but not get "hung up" on self-analysis. We all want to know who we are and how we can succeed. But here's what happens if you keep looking at yourself and asking "How well am I doing?" Either (1) you think you're pretty good, and become a smug, self-satisfied, self-righteous prig, or (2) you think you're pretty bad, and become a head-hanging, unconfident, worried little worm, or (3) you think you're right in the middle, neither hot nor cold but lukewarm, neither black nor white but gray: dull and wishy-washy.

What's the way out? To stop thinking about yourself and think about your neighbors and your God. Eyes are made for looking outward; so are minds. When you get hung up on sin, you get ingrown eyeballs. You also freeze a frown on your face.

All the saints had genuine Christian joy: they found peace and contentment in God's will for their lives. (Read what the apostle Paul wrote in Philippians 4:11–13.) They all struggled mightily with sin. They believed in sin, all right. But they believed even more strongly in God's total forgiveness and omnipotent love (Rom 3: 22–24).

30. What difference does Jesus make to my life?

There is only one person in the world who can answer that question. It is not me, or your parents, or your priest, or even the Pope. It is the person who is reading these words right now.

The difference Jesus *can* make to your life, if you let him, and the difference he *wants* to make, is the difference between being alone and being with God, the difference between trying to play God with your life (and, of course, failing) and letting God be God in your life. It is the difference between despair and hope, the difference between having and not having "a reason to live and a reason to die", the difference between having an ultimate meaning to your life and just letting things drift along and push you around like a leaf on the wind.

Jesus existed long before you were born. "In the beginning was the Word, and the Word was with God, and the Word was God. He was in the beginning with God" (Jn 1:1-2). He said, "Before Abraham was born, I Am" (Jn 8:58). Jesus designed you before you were born; he is the author of your true identity (Ps 139:15-16). Without him you cannot succeed in your life's most important task, knowing who you are and becoming yourself.

Everyone in life has two jobs. Their second jobs vary: mother, ditch digger, president, nurse, auto mechanic, lawyer, shoelace manufacturer, or whatever. Every one of those jobs is replaceable, and, when you die, someone else will do your job in your place. But no one else can ever take your place at your first and most important job in life: being yourself. Only you can do it.

Just as you are unique, one of a kind, Jesus is unique,

one of a kind. Jesus is not one of many alternatives, but the only Savior. He is not for some people and not for others, "for there is one God, and there is one who brings God and mankind together, the man Christ Jesus" (1 Tim 2:5). He is the one bridge from Heaven to earth and from earth to Heaven. "I am the way, the truth, and the life. No one can come to the Father except through me" (Jn 6:14). He brings God into your life and he brings you to God. That's the infinite difference he makes . . . if you let him.

31. What do other religions have in common with Bible teaching?

Vatican Council II told us that there are some profound truths we can learn from other religions, because God has not left the world in darkness, but has given many valuable insights to people in other religions, too, though he has come to earth in person only once, in Christ.

For instance, from Muhammed we can learn the peace that comes from total submission to the will of God. "Islam", the name of Muhammed's religion, means "peace" and "surrender". King David expressed this idea beautifully in Psalm 131.

From Confucius we can learn how social order and harmony in human relationships is the fulfillment of "the will of Heaven", and how practical religion is in working out the details of everyday life in the family and the nation. Psalm 133 and 1 Corinthians 14:33 point out that peace and harmony are what God wants for us.

From Lao Tzu, the founder of Taoism, we can learn the instinctive peaceful wisdom of the "Tao", or "Way of

Nature". You might enjoy reading the *Tao Te Ching*, "the Bible of Taoism": eighty-one short poems about life according to Tao. Parts of it are very similar to the teachings of Jesus, especially in his "Sermon on the Mount" (Mt 5–7).

From Buddha and Hindu teachers we can learn the importance of meditation and silence and stilling the harsh, loud voice of the ego and selfish desire. Buddhists and Hindus are experts in "meditation", and this can be an aid to prayer if used for God and not for our own ends. The Bible commands us to "Be still and know that I am God" (Ps 46:10, KJV). Buddhism cannot teach us to know God as Jesus can, but it can teach us to be still.

We are not told by Jesus or by anything in the Bible how much truth and how much falsehood is to be found in each of the other religions in the world. We *are* told that pagan polytheism (worshiping many gods) and idolatry (worshiping anything instead of God) are totally wrong and false (Ex 20:2–5). We are not told how much of what any other religious teacher said is true. But we are told how much of what Jesus said is true: 100 percent (Jn 1:17; 14:6).

For Jesus is unique. He is not the only religious teacher, or the only wise man, but he is the only man who was God incarnate. He is the only religious teacher who ever claimed to be God, the Creator of the universe born as a human being (Mt 16:13–16; see also Jn 1:1–5, 14). The only other people who ever claimed to be God are not great wise men but insane idiots or blasphemous liars.

Christianity does not mean believing there is no truth in other religions. But it does mean believing Jesus is the One he claims to be. A Christian may believe "there's something in everything." But a Christian must believe that there's everything in Something.

32. Should I believe because my parents believe?

No. If you're old enough to ask that question, you should believe because *you* choose to believe.

The result of faith (belief) is eternal life, God's own life (Jn 6:47). God wants to be your Father. What does a father give to his children first of all? The gift of life, his own kind of life. We already have human life from our human parents. They cannot give us divine life. Only God can do that, and only we can stop him, by refusing it. Each of us must choose yes or no to God's invitation to become his child and join his family.

God has no grandchildren. Never once in the Bible is God called a grandfather, though he is frequently called a Father. Never once is anyone ever called a grandchild of God, but we are all invited to become "God's children" (Jn 1:12–13; Rom 8:14–16). God gives each of us his gift of his own life firsthand, not secondhand. You get God's life yourself from God, not from your parents.

Parents can help, very much, but in the last analysis it's up to you. No matter how many helpers and intermediaries God uses, you are the last link in the chain. God writes the invitation; then his prophets, his Church, your parents, and your teachers all carry it, like mail carriers; but you alone can open the invitation and respond yes or no.

33. How can I meet God?

That's a great question. I hope you really want to know, because we are promised that "anyone who seeks will find", and this is the greatest thing in the world (Mt 7:8).

Meeting God, "knowing" God, not by head knowledge and study alone but by personal experience, by acquaintance, by friendship—this is the point and purpose and end of our lives, and it is our supreme joy. It begins in this life and is perfected in the next. "Eternal life means to know you, the only true God, and to know Jesus Christ, whom you sent" (Jn 17:3). That is the best definition of "eternal life". It is not just more life like this, time without end. It is intimacy with God. It is the "knowledge" that comes only through love.

How do we meet God? Through Jesus. "There is one who brings God and mankind together, the man Christ Jesus" (1 Tim 2:5). We know God by God's "way down", not by any human "way up". "No one has ever seen God. The only Son, who is the same as God and is at the Father's side, he has made him known" (Jn 1:18). To meet God, meet Jesus. Jesus said, "Whoever has seen me has seen the Father" (Jn 14:9).

In turn, we meet Christ through Christians, through Christ's Body, the Church, "the people of God". In reality, the Father is first; Christ the Son eternally comes from him, and then Christ's Church comes at a certain point in time, some two thousand years ago. But we experience these three in reverse order: we learn of Christ through the Church, through Christians; and we learn of the Father through Christ.

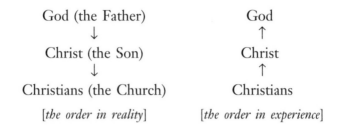

God (the Father)	God
↓	↑
Christ (the Son)	Christ
↓	↑
Christians (the Church)	Christians
[*the order in reality*]	[*the order in experience*]

Christians are like windows through which we meet Christ, and Christ is like the window through which we meet God. But there is one great difference: Christ's window is perfectly clear, while Christians' are usually pretty smudgy and let only a little light through.

Three ways to wash our windows, three ways to let more of the light of Christ shine through our lives, three ways to meet God more intimately, are:

1. by loving him; for you really know people only when you love them. And God is a Person, not a thing.

2. by reading his Word, the Bible (see question 3).

3. by prayer. Ask him! Pray, "God, please let me know you better." And he will.

34. Why can't I find time to pray?

You don't *find* time; you *make* time.

To *make* time for anything, you must *take* that time away from something else. Something must be sacrificed. When you take time to watch television, you sacrifice time to do homework. When you take time to do homework, you sacrifice time to watch television.

Praying means, first of all, sacrificing some time for God. Something else is always bound to come up as soon as you decide to pray. Your mind starts chattering and suggesting a lot of other things you could be doing instead. You must sacrifice these things, at least for a while. The most important part of praying is just this: to decide to give God a block of your time and to stick to that decision.

Something in you shrinks back from prayer. Something in you whispers all sorts of excuses not to pray. That something in you is afraid of prayer. It knows that prayer is practicing the presence of God; and when God is present, he is like light: light destroys its opposite, darkness. So it is patches of darkness in you that fear the light of God, the presence of God, that prayer brings. (Read Jn 3:19–21.)

You must decide: do you listen to those patches of darkness or to God? They are the things God wants to clean up. God is like a house cleaner. Once you let him in, he goes around sweeping and cleaning and washing and rearranging things. And prayer lets him in.

All those things that God wants to rearrange and change in you are causing you guilt and unhappiness. God is not your enemy but your friend, even your lover. His one desire for you (love is very single-minded) is your joy. So you need not fear letting him in to work on you. But "the enemy within", those patches of darkness in you (we all have them), *does* need to fear God. That's why you experience such a reluctance to pray, such a difficulty in praying, especially getting started, even though you may know that prayer is good for you and gives you happiness and peace.

You must decide which voice to listen to.

When a little boy gave Jesus his lunch of five loaves

and two fishes, Jesus multiplied the food to feed five thousand people (Jn 6:1–13). He will do the same with your time. Whatever you give him, he multiplies. When you take time to pray, you will find that you have *more* time left, not less. If this sounds ridiculous to you, I challenge you to try it, with an open mind. I guarantee that you will find in your own experience that it works like that. Take time for God, and the rest of your time will be calmer, more alert, and more efficient. Deny God time, and the rest of your time will be more harried and hassled.

God invented time, created time. He has all the time there is, in his eternity. He is the master and giver of time (Eccl 3:1). If you need more time, you must go to him, where all time is kept. The closer to him you get, the more time you will have; the more you run away from him, the more time will become your master and you will never seem to get enough of it and to "be on top of things".

So you see, prayer is very practical. But we must not pray merely as a practical technique, but out of love and because God deserves it: we pray for the same reason we talk to our friends. God is our First Friend.

On making time for prayer, read Matthew 6:6; Acts 2:42; 3:1; 10:30; and 1 Thessalonians 5:17. For examples of people who took time to pray read 1 Samuel 1:9–2:10 and Tobit 8:4–8.

35. What's the difference between praying and "saying your prayers"?

Perhaps you've seen some situation comedy on television where a very shy boy who can't bring himself to talk directly to this certain girl he's in love with writes out a speech and reads it to her. That's what merely "saying your prayers" is like. If all we do is recite words to God instead of speaking to him directly in our own words, we are like that boy. Sometimes it is because we are shy or afraid. Or it may be because we think of God as distant rather than present, just as you write a letter to your friends when they are far away but not when they are present. But both these reasons are poor ones for (1) God is our friend and lover, not someone to be afraid of, and (2) God is always present, never absent (see Ps 139:1–18).

Formal prayers are fine things, but they should not substitute for personal prayers. What would you think of a friend who never talked directly to you but only read you letters?

The three main uses of formal, pre-written prayers, are (1) for public, group worship, for the sake of unity; (2) as something like songs to sing to God, as you would sing a song to your beloved—*that's* not motivated by fear or shyness or the false idea that you are distant rather than present; and (3) as a beginning for personal prayer, as a sort of runway for the airplane of your own prayer to use to take off from.

Praying is simply talking with God. It's the easiest thing in the world. It's easier than talking with human beings, because there is always the possibility that other human beings will (1) misunderstand us, not really know us, or (2) put us down, not wholly accept us. But God is (1) all-knowing and (2) all-loving. He (1) never misunderstands you, even when you misunderstand yourself. He reads your heart behind your words. And (2) he never puts anyone down. Even when Judas came to betray Jesus, Jesus called him "friend" (Mt 26:50); and he prayed for the Roman soldiers who murdered him, "Forgive them, Father! They don't know what they are doing" (Lk 23:34). That's the kind of God we pray to. If we have sorrows, he knows them. He wept at the grave of his friend Lazarus (Jn 11:35). If we have things in us we do not understand, he understands them all. Even our sins are no obstacle if we repent of them, for he is instantly ready to forgive.

God may sometimes deliberately lead us to the point where words fail us so that we can go beyond words and just rest in his arms (Ps 131). Friends, romantic lovers, and members of a close family often communicate with each other more deeply by silence than by words. Why not try listening to God? You will not hear the words with your ears, but you will hear peace and love with your heart because that is what God is (1 Jn 4:8).

There is no reason in the world why we should fear to be totally open and honest and intimate with God, for "there is nothing in all creation that will ever be able to separate us from the love of God which is ours through Christ Jesus our Lord" (Rom 8:39).

36. How can I see God in my daily life?

First, know he is there. He is not confined to only a few spaces, like church buildings, for *we are* the Church. He is not confined to only a few times, the times of public worship, though that is a special time where he is present in a special way in the Mass, really present in the Eucharist, not just mentally present in the souls of the worshipers. But he is everywhere and everywhen. Therefore it is possible to find him everywhere and everywhen (Jer 23:23).

We can't be consciously aware of God all the time. We shouldn't feel guilty about forgetting about God most of the time; God does not expect us to pray twenty-four hours a day. But we can make everything part of a prayer by offering to God, at the beginning of each day and at the end of each day, all our actions and all our experiences of the day.

The Church sets aside certain times—great liturgical feast days, like Christmas and Easter, every Sunday, and the time for Mass—so that we can charge our spiritual batteries during these times. They are meant to spread into *all* times. For instance, every day of our lives is different because of Easter, because we celebrate and remember and believe in Christ's Resurrection. For "if Christ has not been raised, then your faith is a delusion and you are still lost in your sins" (1 Cor 15:17). Every hour of the day is different because of the Mass, for at Mass we offer to God the perfect prayer and the perfect sacrifice that brings about our salvation and our peace with God, a peace we can be confident of at every minute.

If you are really asking the question "How can I see God in my daily life?" then you will certainly find answers to it. For if that is your desire, God will grant it, for that is what he desires, too (Jer 29:11–13; Rom 12:1–2). You make him very happy by wanting to find him everywhere.

But it takes time to grow, spiritually as well as physically. It is a lifelong learning, an art that we gradually learn better and better. It is practice for Heaven, where the art will be perfected.

Here on earth the best way to do it, I think, is not first of all any one particular technique or "gimmick", but to *want* to with your heart. He promises that all who seek him, find him (Mt 7:7).

37. How should I live?

The first choice everyone has to make is the choice between living blindly, without questioning the meaning of life, or living by seeking the truth. That is the basic difference between an animal and a human being: animals live blindly, by instinct; human beings question and seek the truth. So if you are wondering how to live, you have already partly answered the question how to live. You have chosen to live in a human way, not an animal way: by seeking the truth, not by blind instinct.

To live in a human way is to live by a standard, a set of values, a set of answers to the question: What are the best things in life? Everyone has some set of values, ranked in an order of greater and lesser. For instance, a bank robber has chosen to put a higher value on money than on morality; a martyr has chosen to put a higher value on his faith and his conscience than on his body's self-preservation; one who tells lies to gain power puts power above truth; a mother who refuses to have an abortion puts a higher value on human life than on whatever she has to sacrifice for it.

The most important question you can ask is: What is the most precious thing in your life? What is your greatest good? What is your highest value?

Jesus' answer to that question is: " 'Love the Lord your God with all your heart, with all your soul, and with all your mind.' This is the greatest and the most important commandment. The second most important commandment is like it: 'Love your neighbor as you love yourself' " (Mt 22:37–39).

Everyone worships some god or other, some greatest thing. It may be pleasure, or power, or money, or fame, or being liked, or your job, or your family. Some of these are closer to God than others, but none of them is the very essence of God, and none of them should be the very essence of our life. Jesus went so far as to say that "whoever comes to me cannot be my disciple unless he loves me more than he loves his father and his mother, his wife and his children, his brothers and his sisters, and himself as well" (Lk 14:26). We are to love other people, especially our family, more than anything else, but not more than God. We are to love God with our whole heart and soul, but our neighbor is not God. We cannot love people too much, but we can love God too little. God is first, not second. Not because he is jealous and doesn't like to see us loving anyone else—he *commands* us to love others—but because he knows that if we put anything else in his place, it just won't work. If we put a divine burden on the shoulders of any human being, those shoulders will break and we will be disappointed.

Putting God first does not make human loves less precious. It frees us to love them in a human way. Once our neighbor ceases to be our God, he can truly become our neighbor. And the same is true of everything else in life, every lesser good. Once we have the right scale of values, once we (1) put God above everything, (2) put people above things, and (3) put higher things, like health and happiness, above lower things, like money and bodily pleasures, then everything fits into its natural place.

There is another aspect of the question "How should I live?" that we have not yet looked at. We have asked the question: What should I live *for*? What should my values and ideals be? But we have not asked the question: What should I live *from*? What is the *source* of my living and my strength? It does us no good to have a perfect set of ideals, a perfect map, if we do not have the ability to follow the ideals, to follow the map. There are many good ideals around, and many wise moral teachers who tell you how to live. But they do not give you the power to live by their codes.

Jesus is unique here. He not only tells you how to live, he also gives you the *power* to live his way. That power is the Holy Spirit, God's own spirit really getting inside your soul and giving you the spiritual energy, the ability to live as he wants. This is one way Christianity differs from all mere philosophies and ethical systems. "For the Kingdom of God is not a matter of words but of power" (1 Cor 4:20). God is a dynamo. Touch him, and you will not go away the same.

But how can we touch God? Our reach is not long enough. Our souls cannot stretch to his perfection. But he reached down to us; he became a man to touch us with his power, his own life. That is what Jesus is.

38. Aren't right and wrong up to the individual conscience?

What you *believe* to be right and wrong is indeed up to your own conscience. But what really *is* right and wrong is not. You are not God: you do not *make* a thing right or wrong just by choosing it. The apostle Paul applied this principle to himself in 1 Corinthians 4:3–5.

Right and wrong are not a man-made game. If they were, we would never feel *guilty*. You don't feel guilty when you change the rules of a game you made up.

If moral values were nothing but what I think or what you think, then no one could ever be *wrong* about them. Being wrong means your ideas are different from reality. If there is no reality outside your own ideas, you can never be wrong. For instance, if you write a fictional story, you can't be *wrong* about any detail in that story, because it's all *your* made-up story. But you *can* be wrong about science, or mathematics, or how other people feel, because there is something outside of yourself there, and your ideas about that something might be different from that something.

Morality is something real, not just something made up; something outside our minds, not inside them; something independent of what we think, not something dependent on what we think.

Conscience means what we think and feel about morality. Conscience is our power to understand right and wrong (Rom 9:1). Just as our eyes do not *make* light, our conscience does not *make* right and wrong, but is *aware* of right and wrong.

The ultimate reason why morality is a matter of objective truth, and not just subjective feeling, is because the source of morality is God. He is the Author of the moral law. Even before the Ten Commandments were written down, God impressed on the human conscience the knowledge of right and wrong (Gen 3:1–24). That knowledge is innate. Conscience is God's mouthpiece in our souls (Prov 20:27). That's why we must never ignore our conscience: it is one of God's ways of communicating with us.

However, our conscience is not infallible (Prov 16:25). It can make mistakes. We must test and judge our conscience, therefore, by two other words of God, two other revelations of God, which God *has* guaranteed to be infallible, free from error in all essential matters: the Bible and the Church. Both of these come from Christ, directly or indirectly; that is why they can be infallible. Nothing merely human is infallible. So, if you really want to know what is right and wrong, let your conscience be taught by Christ's two hands that he left on earth to teach us, his Church and his Book. (Read question 8, "How can I know what God wants of me?"; question 10, "What right does the Church have to tell me what to believe and what to do?"; and question 12, "What shall I do with my life?")

We must still decide how to *apply* the laws of God that are taught to us by the Bible and the Church to ever-changing and ever-different situations. We must make our own *use* of the moral tools God has given us. We are given only (1) the moral principles and (2) the moral power, the Holy Spirit. Now we must make our own moral choices (1) to obey or to disobey those principles, and (2) how to apply them to our own lives and our own unique situations. Those are two areas of our freedom. In *that* sense, right and wrong *are* up to the individual conscience. But not in the sense that we can make up our own moral principles, or disobey God's laws and not be morally wrong. (Read Rom 2:12–15; 13:1–5; 1 Cor 10:27–29; 1 Tim 1:19; Titus 1:15; Heb 9:13–14; 10:21–22.)

39. Is anything a sin anymore?

You may doubt whether the old word *sin* is "relevant" in the modern world, since so few people seem to believe in it or take it seriously anymore. The Church used to preach a lot about sin, perhaps too much. The impression pre-Vatican II Catholics often got was that the Christian life was more a matter of avoiding sin than practicing virtue, and that God was more a God of justice than a God of love. Though these things were not *said* (they are heresies, directly contradicting the Church's teaching), they were sometimes implied by teachers who didn't understand the Church's own teachings about good and evil deeply enough. In reaction to that overemphasis on sin, many priests and teachers today go to the opposite extreme and disbelieve in sin or ignore it altogether. But two wrongs don't make a right. One extreme being wrong does not mean the other extreme is right.

God does not change, and his law does not change (Malachi 3:6–7; Mt 5:17–18). *We* change and *our* laws change. The laws and practices of human societies change. But sin does not mean a violation of changing human laws, society's laws. Sin means a violation of God's unchanging law.

It is temptingly easy to justify sin by "Everybody's doing it." But if everybody's sick, that doesn't make sickness health. Poisons that become fashionable do not cease to kill. Isaiah the prophet said to people who thought that way, "You call evil good and call good evil. You turn darkness into light and light into darkness. You make what is bitter sweet, and what is sweet you make bitter" (Is 5:20). We must be honest and call things by their true names. A sin is a sin, no matter what anyone says or does or thinks. A sin is a sin by God's standards, and *they* do not change with the times.

But we should always remember four things when thinking about sin:

1. We are not to judge other people, only actions. "Do not judge others, so that God will not judge you" (Mt 7:1). We should "love the sinner and hate the sin" just as we love our bodies and hate the disease that is its enemy. Sin is the enemy of our souls. We hate sin only because we love human souls.

2. Sin, and its opposite, holiness, are not only a matter of what we do or fail to do; they are also a matter of what we *are*. In theological terms, there is not only "actual sin" (sin*s*) but also "original sin" (the state of sinfulness). Our character is flawed; that is the root of our actions being flawed. God cares more about who we *are* than about how we perform.

78

3. Sin is real but forgiven. "If we say that we have no sin, we deceive ourselves, and there is no truth in us. But if we confess our sins to God, he will keep his promise and do what is right: he will forgive us our sins" (1 Jn 1:8–9). Sin is not the last word: God's forgiving love is the last word.

4. We should think more about good than about evil, more about holiness than about sin, more about success than about failure. We should keep our thoughts filled with good things, not garbage. Solomon said in his Proverbs (4:23): "Be careful how you think; your life is shaped by your thoughts."

40. What is a good person?

There are especially seven qualities that make a good person. They are called "virtues", or strengths of moral character. They have been taught for thousands of years, and so most likely, you have heard of them.

There are, first of all, the four "cardinal" virtues. (*Cardinal* comes from the Latin word *cardo*, which means "hinge": these four are the ones on which all other virtues hinge, or depend.) They are (1) justice, or fairness; (2) prudence, or wisdom; (3) fortitude, or courage; and (4) moderation, or self-control (Wis 8:7). Justice means basically the "Golden Rule": "Do for others what you want them to do for you" (Mt 7:12). Prudence means basically understanding people and situations, understanding what is needed (Hos 14:9). Fortitude means the guts to stand up for what is right and to resist wrong, even when it is hard to do that (Eph 6:10–20). And moderation means to control your desires and animal appetites by reason, to overcome greed and selfishness (Gal 5:19–25).

There are also the three "theological", or God-centered, virtues: faith, hope, and charity, or love (1 Cor 13:13). These are the vertical virtues; the four cardinal virtues are the horizontal virtues. The theological virtues make us right with God; the cardinal virtues make us right with ourselves and our neighbors.

Faith means believing in what God has revealed because we believe in God. Hope means believing God's promises; it is faith applied to the future. And charity means self-giving love, self-forgetful love.

41. How can I become a better person?

The description of a good person in the preceding question (the seven virtues) is appealing. No one likes a person who is unfair, foolish, cowardly, out of control, cynical, despairing, and hating. Everyone loves a person who is fair, wise, courageous, self-controlled, faithful, hopeful, and loving. But how can you become such a person?

There are two essentials: you and God. You can't do it without him and he won't do it without you. Cooperation is the way. It's like a marriage: each party gives 100 percent. It's not 50–50, you doing half and God doing half. You can do *nothing* without him (he said exactly that in John 15:5), and he will do nothing without you.

There are some practical helps, too, such as:

1. Trusting does more than trying (Prov 3:5–6).

2. First things first: God first, love first (Mt 22:36–39).

3. Become sensitive to the voice of conscience, and act as soon as you feel conscience nudging you. Give yourself no time to make excuses.

4. Offer your thinking to God as well as your acting, for all our acting comes from our thoughts. Saint Paul says "we take every thought captive and make it obey Christ" (2 Cor 10:5).

5. It's hard to do it alone. Christian friends reinforce each other. So do companions in sin. Never be a snob, but seek out *good* friends. A true friend is someone who helps you, and if your friends get you into trouble with God, they are not true friends. (Read Prov 17:17 and 1 Thess 5:11.)

6. Be utterly honest with yourself and with God (Prov 2:6–8). It's harder than you think. We love to flatter and fool ourselves.

7. Above all, pray (Phil 4:6–7). God is the source of all goodness, and we get close to him in prayer. Prayer can change the world. Prayer can change your life.

42. Do I have to obey my parents?

You know you do. Your conscience tells you so. So does the fourth commandment: "Respect your father and your mother" (Ex 20:12). And Ephesians 6:1 says "It is your Christian duty to obey your parents, for this is the right thing to do." Paul considers disobedience of parents to be a serious sin. In Romans 1:28–32 and 2 Timothy 3:2–9, people who disobey their parents are listed among those who are opposed to the true knowledge of God.

That does not mean your parents are never wrong. They are not infallible. Often they make mistakes. Often they show their faults, just as you do. There is no way to avoid all fault and sin in human relationships, but there is a way to deal with faults; it's called forgiveness. And that works both ways: both parties in any relationship must be ready to forgive.

God put your parents over you to help you, not to harm you; for your sake, not for their sake. Most of their work is giving (2 Cor 12:14). It's hard work.

When you think your parents are being unreasonable and asking too much of you, you must still obey them, unless you can convince them to change their minds (and you do that best by being reasonable, not by sulking or screaming). If you were free to follow your own mind instead of theirs, you wouldn't need them in the first place.

The only time it is right to deliberately disobey your parents is when they tell you to do something that you honestly believe is morally wrong. That is a very rare situation. But when God and humans disagree, we must obey God rather than humans.

What about when your parents disagree with each other and tell you different things? That is a hard situation. Especially when parents are divorced, they often try to pull children in opposite directions. Please try not to blame them too much for that; it's very hard not to do that. And please do not think that you are somehow responsible for your parents' difficulties or divorce in the first place. It is almost never true that children are to blame for their parents' troubles.

If your father is gone, by death or divorce or separation, God can still be your father. And if your mother is gone, God can also be your mother. For he invented both fathers and mothers. Jesus also gave us his own mother to be our own (cf. Jn 19:26).

(For more about respect for and obedience to parents, read Prov 1:8–9, 6:20, 13:1, and 15:5. See also Col 3:20.)

43. Can a Christian be in the military?

Neither the Bible nor the Church gives a final answer to this question, so it is up to your individual conscience.

John the Baptist, the last Old Testament prophet, who pointed out Jesus as the Messiah, told the soldiers who came to him for advice: "Don't take money from anyone by force or accuse anyone falsely. Be content with your pay" (Lk 3:14), but he did not tell them to leave the army. On the other hand, Jesus warned that "all who take the sword will die by the sword" (Mt 26:52).

The Catholic Church's teachings on war say that there is such a thing as a just war, and the military is an honorable profession if it serves justice. A just war is essentially a war that is (1) defensive rather than offensive, and (2) necessary to prevent a greater evil. But the Church also teaches that pacifism, the refusal to use violence for national defense, is also an honorable option for a Catholic (Rom 12:17–21). There were many Christian pacifists in the early Church.

If you enter the military, it should be for the right motive: for peace (Mt 5:9). That is the only reason that justifies the existence of the military, for wars are justly fought only to make peace. Wars are for the sake of ending wars. War is a horrible, barbaric practice. Pope Paul VI called out to the world, like a prophet, to outlaw all war forever. If you go into the military, it should be with this motive: to help *end* war and to risk your life, if necessary, to save innocent lives.

44. What does God think of suicide?

If suicide is murder—murdering yourself—then suicide is contrary to biblical principles, and *never* what God wants for anyone.

According to Scripture, you are supposed to love yourself as well as your neighbor (Lev 19:18). If you must "love your neighbor as you love yourself", then you must love yourself as you love your neighbor. You do not love someone when you murder him. You do not love yourself when you kill yourself. Exodus 20:13 forbids murder.

Although suicide is a sin, it is not unforgivable. We must not despair of a suicide's salvation. But we must not glorify or idealize it either. Only God knows the state of a suicide's soul (or anyone else's for that matter). Only God can judge (Heb 4:13).

People who attempt suicide are people who have given up—who feel overwhelmed by depression or problems in their lives. They are people who have taken their eyes off the great lover and healer of their souls. They have taken their eyes off God. To hope again, they have to look to him again (Ps 34:18).

If you or someone you know is contemplating suicide, let me encourage you to seek help. God often works through people, and he can work through people who care about you to help you through your tough times. Talking with your priest or with a parent, a teacher, or a friend may give you a fresh perspective on how to approach difficulties. Their support may fill you with the courage you need to keep going. Give them the chance to love you, because when you know you are loved, you do not want to die.

45. Is it sinful to be rich?

No. Jesus had rich friends, for instance Lazarus, whom he raised from the dead.

But it is both sinful and foolish to lust after riches or to worry about money and to fear not having enough. Jesus said that very clearly in his famous "Sermon on the Mount" (see Mt 6:19–34). He talked very often about money, and said that "you cannot serve both God and money" (Mt 6:24).

You can be rich and yet not *attached* to your riches, not a slave of your money (1 Tim 6:17–19); but it is hard. Jesus said, "I assure you: it will be very hard for rich people to enter the Kingdom of Heaven" (Mt 19:23). Riches are a strong temptation; they tend to distract people from God. Rich people have extra problems and extra responsibilities, both to God and their neighbors. It is foolish to long to be rich (1 Tim 6:9–10). Riches do not bring happiness. Neither does power. But both can be used for God. It is not wrong to desire riches and power as *means* to the end of doing good works and helping other people. But most people desire riches as an *end*, for themselves, not to give away.

The best thing about having money is being able to

give it away. But we all have something right now that is much better than money to give away, something our friends need more than money: our love. If you have love, you are rich. And love, unlike money, does not diminish when it is given away. Just the opposite: it increases.

My friend's rich father died and left him a lot of money. Someone said to him, "Now you are a rich man." My friend replied, "No, now I am a poor man: I have no father." My friend is a wise man.

46. Is rock music evil?

Music is one of God's greatest gifts. Music can be a form of prayer (Eph 5:19; Col 3:16).

But any good thing *can* be turned to bad uses. While rock music, of course, is not specifically addressed in the Bible, there is a Bible principle that can be applied to determine whether it is evil. The principle to use in judging such things is Jesus' principle. He said, in Matthew 7:16–18, "You will know them by their fruits. Are grapes gathered from thorns, or figs from thistles? So, every sound tree bears good fruit, but the bad tree bears evil fruit. A sound tree cannot bear evil fruit, nor can a bad tree bear good fruit."

If rock music's fruits, or results, for you are happiness and healthy attitudes, then it is not evil for you. If its fruits are anger or violence or depression or rebellion or withdrawal from life or drugs or sexual promiscuity, then it is evil for you.

Many rock lyrics explicitly attack religion, and glorify drugs, violence, and "free" sex (i.e., *enslavement* to sex as to a drug). Some are even explicitly Satanic, promoting demon-worship. But this does not mean that all rock music is evil. Many books do these things, too, but that doesn't mean we should condemn all books.

If you wonder whether rock music is evil, pray about it; then follow your conscience. If you can't pray about it, if you can't bring it into the presence of God, then leave it alone. That goes for anything.

47. Is alcohol sinful?

The same principles apply here as in the question on rock music. We must judge a thing by its fruits.

Alcohol is not sinful in itself. It is not wrong to use it in moderation. Jesus drank wine. In fact, his first miracle was to make wine out of water (Jn 2). And he used wine as one of the two materials of the Eucharist, the holiest thing in the world (Mt 26:27–29; Mk 14:23–25). The Psalmist prayed to God, "You make grass grow for the cattle and plants for man to use, so that he can grow his crops and produce wine to make him happy" (Ps 104:14–15).

But alcoholic beverages do not always make us happy. They make millions of people very unhappy. Millions are chemically or psychologically enslaved to alcohol. It is the most common deadly factor in fatal auto accidents, domestic violence, broken homes, and violent assaults, and figures in many murders and suicides. It may not be bad in itself, but it is very bad for very many people.

Some individuals seem to have very little problem with alcohol; others have great problems. The practical rule is, "Better safe than sorry." The Bible contains many warnings against drunkenness. See, for example, Proverbs 20:1, 23:21; Romans 13:13; 1 Corinthians 5:11, 6:9–10; Ephesians 5:18; 1 Peter 4:3. If you find yourself using alcohol immoderately, you may already have a problem or be headed for one. Master it before it masters you. "Immoderate use" means either "to the point of drunkenness" or "unable to leave it alone".

"Your body is the temple of the Holy Spirit" (1 Cor 6:19). Anything that harms our bodies is wrong. If no harm is done, we are free to enjoy all the good things God put on this earth for us.

48. What does God think about sex?

That is the right question. What *we* think about anything is not the standard by which we should measure what God thinks about it, but vice versa.

God invented sex. One of the first commands God gave to mankind was "Have many children" (Gen 1:28). So if we want to find out what it is and how to use it, we'd better listen to its inventor.

1. First of all, sex is not just something you can *do* but something you *are*. Sexuality (maleness, femaleness) is God's design (Gen 1:27). It is a quality of your personality, not just an act of your reproductive organs. You *are* either a man or a woman. You don't have to "have sex" to be sexually fulfilled. Jesus was sexually fulfilled, sexually complete, without "having sex". So was his virgin mother Mary.

2. Sex is not something to "get". It is designed for giving (Song of Solomon 7:11–13). Total sex is total self-

giving. But it is impossible to give the *whole* of yourself to more than one person. If you want the most perfect, total, and joyful sex possible for any human being, then you want monogamy, sexual fidelity, sex for the one person you give the whole of yourself to in marriage (Prov 5:15).

Marriage personalizes sex. Sex with many people, promiscuous sex, means depersonalized sex. The person then is a means to sexual pleasure as an end. Different means can be used for the same end, so different persons can be used for sexual pleasure. In sexual promiscuity, you love sexual pleasure as your end. The other person is the means. But in marriage the other person is your end; you love *him or her sexually*, rather than loving sex as such.

3. One of the obvious natural ends, or purposes, of sexual intercourse is having children (Gen 1:28). God designed it to produce babies *and* to give pleasure. We can rip up his design and artificially separate the two things he designed to be naturally together. One way to do this is by test tube babies or cloning (cloning is not yet scientifically possible but probably will be one day), which gives you babies without sexual intercourse. The other way is artificial contraception, which gives you sexual intercourse without babies.

The purpose of contraception is to get pleasure without getting babies. It is called "birth control" but is really birth *prevention*. Contraception is like the ancient Roman vomitorium, where rich people went to throw up one meal so they could eat another one right away: they separated the pleasure of eating from its natural purpose, nutrition, just as contraception separates the pleasure of sexual intercourse from its natural purpose, reproduction.

The Roman Catholic Church has always condemned artificial contraception as unnatural and wrong. The fact that it is very widely used, even among Catholics, does not make it right. Many other wrong things (pride, greed, selfishness) are also very popular, but that does not turn them into right things.

4. Sexual love between people who have chosen to give the whole of themselves to each other in marriage is meant to be one of the most wonderful experiences in human life (Prov 5:18–19). Our society is so sex-saturated partly because it is desperately searching for the joy in sex that it instinctively knows is there but which it does not find. And it does not find that joy because it looks for it in the wrong place: in *unnatural* sex, either (1) a merely external, materialistic sex, sex as something merely to *do*, not to *be*; or (2) selfish sex, sex as something to *have*, to get, not to give; or (3) partial sex, sex with more than one person; or (4) artificial, held-back sex, contraceptive sex versus reproduction. Our plastic, cheap, fast-food society has cheapened sex into a kind of plastic, fast-food commodity. God's plan here, as everywhere, is more wise and loving than ours. If we follow his way, we will find the *real* "joy of sex".

Sex is not the most important thing in life. But there is no area of life in the modern world where the wisdom of God more obviously contradicts the "wisdom" of the world. And there is no area of modern life where the "wisdom" of the world is more fouled up. If the world had attained sexual happiness and joy and contentment

McCoy Church Goods Co, Inc
1010 Howard Ave
San Mateo, CA 94401
650-342-0924

INVOICE #   145169
01/18/08 11:46:48 AM

9780898704884
  YOUR QUESTIONS,   1x 11.95*

Subtotal: 11.95
Tax: 0.99
CASH SALE   12.94

Total: 12.94

Amt Tendered: 13.04
Change: 0.10
Legend * = Taxable
Entered By KENDI
    Thank You for Shopping at
   McCoy Church Goods Co, Inc

Receipt required for any returns
        within 30 days.

        GIFT RECEIPT
INVOICE #   145169   01/18/08

    McCoy Church Goods Co, Inc
        1010 Howard Ave
      San Mateo, CA 94401
         650-342-0924
           HOURS:
Mon thru Fri: 9am-5pm, Sat: 9am-1pm

in its way, it would not be so desperately seeking and so desperately worried about sex. It's when the pipes are leaking that you see a lot of books on plumbing. God's book is the only one that works.

49. What does God think about divorce?

That is the right question again. For what God thinks about us is even more important than what we think about God, because what God thinks must be true, while what we think is not always true. If we always ask this first question first, the question about what God thinks, then our own thinking will be right.

Jesus clearly announced God's plan about marriage: it is for life. No divorce. (See Mt 5:31–32, 19:1–12; Mk 10:11–12; Lk 16:18.)

If a Catholic marriage goes sour, then, what are the options available? (1) Marry someone else outside the Church, which is adultery; (2) separate without remarriage (this is tragic but allowable); or (3) heal the torn marriage, which is certainly the best option.

("Annulment", which the Church allows, is not divorce. It is a declaration that there never was a marriage in the first place. You cannot get an annulment just because you are no longer in love.)

Nearly everyone in our society has been touched by the tragedy of divorce or knows someone who has. We must be compassionate and forgiving to those hurt by divorce, but it is not compassionate to say that this terrible thing is all right. The Church's total ban on divorce is really compassionate, not cruel, for Catholics who believe and obey the Church's teaching have a life-long guarantee in marriage.

The Roman Catholic Church is under pressure to change her teaching forbidding divorce, but she *cannot* do so. For one thing, it would not be truly compassionate to allow this uncompassionate thing. For another thing, the Church cannot change her teaching because she must remain faithful to Jesus Christ, her Lord, no matter how strong the pressures from society to compromise. What the Church gives us is not just a teaching she has invented—she can change any of the teachings she has invented, like laws about fasting, holy days of obligation, and whether priests can marry or not—but she gives us the teaching of Christ. When we choose to obey or disobey her, we are choosing to say Yes or No *to Jesus Christ*. "Jesus said to his disciples, 'Whoever listens to you listens to me; whoever rejects you rejects me'" (Lk 10:16).

There are many complex and difficult aspects of divorce. How then can the Catholic Church be so simple and absolute, so black-and-white, so yes-or-no, about a situation that is not simple? The answer is that the Church does not get her principles and standards from the situation, from the world, which is changing and uncertain, but from God, who is eternal and absolute. She does not have the authority to correct her Lord.

50. Is homosexuality sinful?

Heterosexuals, or "straights", should not single out homosexuals, or "gays", as worse sinners than they are. Saint Paul, in Romans 1, lists many sins that the human race is guilty of. Among them is homosexual activity. But then, in the next chapter, he warns us not to condemn others because we are sinners, too: "Do you, my friend, pass judgment on others? You have no excuse at all, whoever you are" (Rom 2:1). We must hate the sin, but love the sinner, just as God does to us.

The Catholic Church distinguishes two different aspects of homosexuality. *Homosexuality* is not a sin, but homosexual *acts* are sins. Homosexual *acts* are sins, but a homosexual *orientation* as an uncontrollable *feeling or desire* for sexual intercourse with a member of the same sex rather than the opposite sex may be a psychological *disease* or disorder, but the orientation in itself is not a sin because it is not a free *choice*. We are responsible for how we act as well as the thoughts we *choose* to think about, for that is up to our free choice; but we are not directly responsible for how we feel. Homosexuals may not be able to help the way they feel. It is wrong to look down on them as sinful just because of how they feel.

But the Bible clearly teaches, from beginning to end, that homosexual intercourse is wrong, is contrary to God's will (Gen 19:4–8, 24–25; Lev 18:22, 20:13; Rom 1:24, 26–27; 1 Cor 6:9). God designed us to find sexual fulfillment with someone of the opposite sex, not someone of the same sex.

There may be physical, genetic causes of homosexuality, but God does not force anyone to be an active homosexual. God's work is always to liberate people from all kinds of evil: physical, psychological, moral, and spiritual. When Jesus was on earth, he showed the nature of God more perfectly and clearly than anyone else ever could. If you want to know what God is like, you must look at Jesus. He said, "Whoever has seen me has seen the Father" (Jn 14:9). And what did Jesus do? He healed diseases, all diseases—diseases of the body, like blindness, diseases of the mind and feelings, like guilt, and the disease of the spirit called sin.

If you have homosexual desires, please know that Jesus loves you no less and wants to help you. "He forgives all my sins and heals all my diseases" (Ps 103:3). But to be helped, we must do three things. First, we must admit that we need to be helped. For as Jesus said, "People who are well do not need a doctor, but only those who are sick" (Lk 5:31). Second, we must believe he can help us to abstain from homosexual acts and we must trust him, for "for God everything is possible" (Mt 19:26). (See Mk 9:22–24.) Third, we must ask him, for he has promised, "Ask, and you will receive" (Mt 7:7).

Homosexuals often justify their behavior as right. The only way you can do that if you believe the Bible to be God's Word is by ignoring or changing the clear teaching in the Bible that homosexual acts are wrong. Heterosexuals may wonder how homosexuals can possibly do this, since the Bible is so clear here. But heterosexuals just as often do the same kind of thing, for instance about the Bible's teaching about sex outside of marriage. It is easy to rationalize and justify something we have a strong passion and desire for; passion blinds the reason and creates a strong prejudice.

Homosexuals have a hard task in life: to resist the sexual temptations that keep coming to them. But heterosexuals also have to resist sexual temptations, as well as the temptation to judge and condemn homosexuals as persons. Remember what Jesus said to the people who were condemning the prostitute (Jn 8:7): "Whichever one of you has committed no sin may throw the first stone at her."

There is a wonderful organization for homosexuals who want to be faithful Catholics. It is called "Courage". Your bishop or pastor can tell you where the nearest local chapter is.

51. Is lust a sin?

Jesus says it is (Mt 5:27).

You must choose: do you judge *him* by what *you* feel, or like, or wish, or think? Or vice versa?

Most people misunderstand the meaning of the word *lust*. They think it means simply strong sexual desire, or passion. And since this is natural and normal, they think Christianity teaches that something natural and normal is sinful.

But lust does not mean simply sexual *desire*, but *deliberately inflaming* your sexual desire for a woman or man who is not your wife or husband, or deliberately planning to commit adultery with them. (Consider the story of David and Bathsheba in 2 Samuel 11 and Shechem's rape of Dinah as recorded in Genesis 34.)

We are justly praised or blamed only for the good or evil things that we freely choose, not for the feelings and instincts that arise in us without our free choice. For instance, when you see a very attractive person of the opposite sex, your head naturally turns and your heart beats fast. That is not lust. But if you then start to command your mind to fantasize about what it would feel like to go to bed with that person, that is lust. Lust can also manifest itself in masturbation. This is not sex as God intended it to be.

Lust is a sin, but it is far from the worst sin. We should not rationalize and deceive ourselves that it is not a sin, but we should not be hung up on it and feel *overly* guilty about it either, as if it is the worst sin in the world. The cold, deliberate, spiritual sins are far worse, like envy, hatred, resentment, greed, pride, and arrogance. You are not a terrible person if you have a problem with lust; you are just a normal sinner. Many of the great saints, like Saint Augustine, had hang-ups in this area. The best way to overcome a hang-up is to get your mind on other things (Philippians 4:8 lists good things to think about). There's more to life than sex.

52. How can I control my sexual desires?

Here is what God's Word says about our question. It is essentially this: remember who you are, a child of God, and remember the price God paid for you: the blood of his Son. "The man who is guilty of sexual immorality sins against his own body. Don't you know that your body is the temple of the Holy Spirit, who lives in you and who was given to you by God? You do not belong to yourselves but to God; he bought you for a price. So use your bodies for God's glory" (1 Cor 6:18–20).

Here are some pieces of practical advice:

1. You can't control desires, which arise within you without your free choice; but you can control what you do about them. Desires are your raw material; your

choice to follow them or not is the work of art that you make of your life (2 Tim 2:22).

2. Sex is not the most important thing in the world; sexual pleasure is not the greatest pleasure in the world; and sexual sin is not the greatest sin in the world. These three myths are widely believed; and when they are, they foster an obsession with sex that is simply silly.

3. Our society is more sexually obsessed than any other society in history. Don't let yourself be cowed and bullied by it. We are not living in a Christian society. We do not take our standards from this society. We march to a different drummer.

4. Realize that your society wants to keep you in a state of sexual desire because it sells things that way. An addict has little sales resistance.

5. A sense of humor helps dissipate an obsession. Sex is one of the funniest things in the world, not the swoony-sweaty-serious thing that half our movies make it out to be.

6. If we want to control our desires, sexual or other, we must begin where desires begin: in our thoughts. "Sow a thought, reap an act. Sow an act, reap a habit. Sow a habit, reap a character. Sow a character, reap a destiny." We must take our thoughts captive and give them to Christ (2 Cor 10:5).

7. We must emphasize the positive, not the negative. The ideal of a clean, free, brave, honest child of God should move us to act according to that ideal (Prov 29:6).

8. The sacrament of Penance (Confession) is there for our sake, for forgiveness when we fail. We will probably fail frequently in this area. But Jesus came for failures,

not for successes. Doctor Jesus came for the sick, not for the well (Lk 5:30–32). Penance is his treatment.

9. When you feel alone, it is much harder to overcome sexual temptation than when you realize Jesus is there with you (Mt 28:20). The practice of the presence of Christ sheds a light and a power on any situation. Stay close to Jesus through the sacrament of the Eucharist. He is the light who dispels the darkness. The closer you are to him, the more light will be in your life. The more you ignore or run away from him, the more darkness you will get into.

10. Human friends also help or hinder, encourage or tempt. Be sure your friends really *are* your friends, helpers not hinderers (Heb 10:24–25).

11. Read God's Word every day. It is not just any book; it reveals God's power (Rom 1:16). God meets you and strengthens you through his Word. Read it as a prayer.

53. Is abortion always wrong?

The Catholic Church has always taught that abortion is murder: killing an innocent human being. An unborn baby is certainly innocent, and it (rather, *he* or *she*) is a human being, not an "it". And abortion means killing him or her. To call it "terminating a pregnancy" is simply dishonest and evasive language.

No matter how hard the alternative to murder is, no matter what society allows you to do, and no matter what the circumstances of your situation may be, murder is never right. In considering abortion, the alternative is often very hard: nine months of an unwanted pregnancy. And society says "Do it." The U.S. Supreme Court made abortion legal with its *Roe vs. Wade* decision, just as that same Supreme Court said slavery is legal and that a black man is only three-fifths of a human being with its *Dred Scott* decision in the last century.

The Supreme Court is not infallible. But God is. And God says, simply, "Do not commit murder" (Ex 20:13).

The Church is not being hard and tough and unfeeling when she strictly forbids abortion. She is being kind and compassionate and loving when she does this. Jesus always sided with the weak, the oppressed, the poor, and the defenseless. No one is more defenseless and weak than an unborn baby.

From the moment of conception each baby is a separate and distinct human individual, with his or her own genetic code, which decides which sex, eye color, temperament, body shape, and many other features that person will have right from the beginning. There is no clear dividing line after the moment of conception, but only gradual growth. You did not become a human being only when your umbilical cord was cut, or at the moment when your head first came out of your mother's womb, or three or six months after conception; you were a human individual from the beginning, from conception. That is a scientific fact. Just as a baby moth is a baby moth from the moment of its conception, a baby human being is a baby human being, and not something else, from its beginning. It is not a fish or an ape or a tumor. And it is not part of the mother. If it were, then the mother would have four legs, four arms, and four eyes!

God created us in his image, with souls (Gen 1:27; 2:7). That is why human life is sacred. That is why murder is wrong. Many people in our society no longer believe this. Instead of a "sanctity of life" ethic, they believe in a "quality of life" ethic: that you are a human being, with human rights, including the right to life, the right not to be killed, only if the quality of your life is high enough (and who's to say what "high enough" is?), for instance if you have a high enough I.Q., and if you are not too severely handicapped. Nothing could be farther from the philosophy of Jesus.

Mother Teresa says that abortion kills twice: it kills the body of the baby and the conscience of the mother. Women who abort their babies feel great guilt years afterward. Abortion exploits and harms women.

What would you think of a person who killed his pet cat or dog because he did not want him, instead of giving him to his neighbor who offered to take him and care for him and love him? There are tens of thousands of loving couples who cannot have a baby of their own but want very much to adopt one. They have to wait for years, usually, and sometimes for nothing, because there are very few babies available for adoption, because millions are destroyed by abortion instead. Adoption is a far better solution to an unwanted pregnancy than murder. Adoption helps (1) the baby by keeping it alive; and it helps (2) the mother's conscience and respect for life; and it helps (3) the new parents to be happy by giving them what they want more than anything else in the world— a baby to love.

54. What do I say if people challenge my beliefs?

Catholics are commanded by Saint Peter (1 Pet 3:15–16) to "be ready at all times to answer anyone who asks you to explain the hope you have in you, but do it with gentleness and respect."

God does not need us; he can work on the hearts of people who do not yet believe, and he can do this directly. But he prefers to do it indirectly, through us. He works through human means. We the Church are the Body of Christ, Christ's hands and feet and mouth (1 Cor 12:12–31).

The last group of questions in this book are all about giving reasons for your faith. Here are seven suggestions about how to do that, in general. The next ten questions will deal with specific issues.

1. You will get nowhere unless both you and the other person are committed to truth and honesty. The only honest reason anyone should ever believe *anything* is because it is true. If one party believes in truth and the other party does not, no real dialogue can take place.

2. If you cannot reason with your neighbors in a spirit of love, it is better not to reason with them at all. God himself says, "Come now, let us reason together" (Is 1:18, literal translation). "I win, you lose" arguments are doomed, for even when you win them, you lose your neighbor. You want to win *your neighbor*, not the *argument*, first of all (1 Cor 9:19–22).

3. People only listen to a listener. Let your neighbor give his reasons for his beliefs. Listen, sincerely. Ask him questions. Be his student, let him be your teacher, at first. Then find the weakness in what he believes and

ask questions about that. Be interested in his beliefs and he may be interested in yours. Read Acts 17:16–34 to see how Saint Paul used this method.

4. Your reasons for your faith need not be scientific proofs. When we're talking about *people*, and reasons for trusting people, we don't expect scientific proofs, just good reasons, good clues. We demand scientific proofs only for things in nature. But God is not a thing in nature. He is a Person who created nature (Gen 1:1–2:4).

5. Don't rely on your own cleverness, but on God. "If the LORD does not build the house, the work of the builders is useless" (Ps 127:1). That applies to buildings made of ideas (arguments) as well as buildings made of bricks (houses). All we can do is to provide tools for God to use. He works on people's hearts. We cannot convert anyone, only God can. But we can sow seeds for God to give growth to.

6. Don't be afraid to reason with an unbeliever, no matter how much smarter you may think he is. You have something unconquerable on your side: truth. There can never be a valid argument against the Catholic faith. There can never be a real contradiction between faith and reason, or faith and science, or faith and logic. All truth is God's truth, and God cannot contradict himself.

7. Remember that people are moved by their hearts more than by their heads. Show them the God of love, and they will *want* to believe in him. People disbelieve mainly because they misunderstand and fear: they may think God is a kind of celestial bank manager, or bookkeeper, or policeman. The world was converted by twelve peasants who *showed* them God.

People didn't first prove the existence of God, then the divinity of Christ, then the divine authority of the Church. It was the other way round. People first met Christians, the Church, and their reaction was, "Whatever those people have, we want." The Christians said, "It's Jesus." Then after knowing Christ through Christians, they came to know God through Christ. It still happens that way.

Faith is a wonderful thing to share. It brings joy, and joy is doubled when it is shared. But one way to share it is honest reasoning.

55. How can I be sure God is real?

If someone asks you *why* you believe in God, what do you reply? Here are ten good reasons for believing in God.

1. *The First Cause Argument.* The universe is a series of causes, like an enormous, complicated set of dominoes, one knocking another down. If nothing moved the first domino, the whole chain of dominoes could not move. If there's no First Cause, there can't be second and third and fourth causes.

Most scientists now believe that the universe was not always here. Fifteen billion years ago, all of matter and space and time began in an explosion scientists call the "Big Bang". It could not happen by itself. A "Big Bang" needs a "Big Banger".

The Bible uses the first cause argument. Romans 1:20 says that God's "eternal power and his divine nature . . . are perceived in the things that God has made." Saint

Paul condemned idolaters because "instead of worshiping the immortal God, they worship images made to look like mortal man or birds or animals or reptiles" (Rom 1:23), whose existence demanded a greater Creator. They should have known better.

2. *The Argument from Design.* This argument takes the first one a step further: not only must the universe have been caused, but its design implies an intelligent, purposeful Designer.

If you found a stone hut on a desert island, you would not explain it by chance, but by intelligent design: you would think a person built it, not the wind. But the universe has in it a far more complex design than any part of it has. The Mind that designed the universe must be infinitely wiser than any human mind. We can design a work of art, but can we design a universe?

An unbeliever was arguing with a believer that the whole universe just happened by chance. Later, the two of them were in a store, and the unbeliever was admiring a painting. "Who painted that?" he asked. "No one", answered the believer. "It just happened by chance."

In the Scriptures, the order of the universe bears witness to God (Ps 19:1–6). "He has always given evidence of his existence by the good things he does: he gives you rain from Heaven and crops at the right times; he gives you food and fills your hearts with happiness" (Acts 14:17).

3. *The Argument from Miracles.* Only a supernatural Being, with supernatural power, could perform a supernatural act, a miracle. In Bible times "God added his witness . . . by performing all kinds of miracles and wonders" (Heb 2:4). And there is abundant evidence for

miracles really happening, not only in Bible times but throughout history and even today, to anyone who investigates with an open mind. (See question 56.)

4. *The Argument from Conscience.* Everyone knows he ought always to obey his conscience, no matter what. Even unbelievers have a conscience (Rom 2:14–15). And conscience speaks with absolute authority. It is not like the rules of a game.

Now where did this absolute authority come from? Nothing in us is absolute, so how could we be the author of conscience? Society is only more creatures like ourselves; adding billions of only relative authorities still does not give you an absolute authority. Only an absolute will explains the absolute authority of conscience. Conscience is the voice of God.

5. *The Argument from Consequences.* The consequences of faith in God are hope and joy and a life full of meaning: "a reason to live and a reason to die." The consequences of unbelief are ultimate emptiness and despair. "Fools say to themselves, 'There is no God!'" (Ps 14:1, 53:1).

6. *The Argument from Love.* Love is the greatest of miracles. How could an evolved ape create the noble idea of self-giving love? Human love is a result of our being made to resemble God (Gen 1:26–27; James 3:9), who himself is love (1 Jn 4:8). If we are made in the image of King Kong rather than in the image of King God, where do the saints come from?

7. *The Argument from History.* A wise student of history can see God's providential hand. History is *his*-story. It shows a divine design. You can see this divine order in the history of Israel in the Old Testament, and perhaps

also in your own life. (This is not so much an argument as an awareness, or an invitation to look.)

8. *The Experiential Argument.* If you have an honest, scientific mind, an open mind, then you must test every theory fairly. The fair test of the "theory" of God is to pray. If you want to know whether God exists or not, go out into your back yard at midnight, look up at the sky, and say, "God, I don't know whether you are real or not, but I want to know. If you do exist and love me and want me to know you, then here I am. I am open to you, open to the truth. Please let me know you are real, in your own way and your own time." No honest person could quarrel with that experiment. But if anyone sincerely prays that prayer, he will not be an atheist for long. Of that fact we are guaranteed by God himself: "Anyone who seeks will find" (Mt 7:8). The best "argument" with unbelievers is just to get them to seek. God will take care of the rest.

9. *The Argument from Beauty.* I know three ex-atheists who have told me, independently of each other, that the main reason they decided to believe in God was the music of Johann Sebastian Bach. "If there is Bach, there must be God." (You either just see that, or you don't.)

10. The best argument for God is *Jesus.* "In many and various ways God spoke of old to our Fathers by the prophets, but in these last days he has spoken to us by a Son" (Heb 1:1–2). Meet him. Read the Gospels. Then you will know God: "Whoever has seen me has seen the Father", says Jesus (Jn 14:9). Jesus is the transparent window to the Father. Almost no one who reads the Gospels can avoid being deeply impressed by Jesus, as a man, at least. But if there is no God, then Jesus was

the biggest fool who ever walked this earth, because no one ever pinned more of his whole life and its meaning onto God.

Jesus' disciples gave *reasons* for their faith (e.g., Acts 19:8); but, much more effectively, they also gave *witness* to their faith (e.g., Acts 2:32). Their answer, the Church's answer, to the question "How do you know that God is real?" is this: "I have met him, and I bear him witness."

Sometimes God says, "Come, let us reason together." (Is 1:18), but sometimes he just says, "Come and see" (Jn 1:39).

56. Can't you just believe in Christian values without believing in miracles?

All of the most important events in the Bible are miracles: the Creation; God's founding of his chosen people through Abraham; the Exodus; the giving of the law, the Ten Commandments; the prophets; the Virgin Birth and Incarnation of Jesus; Jesus' life, full of miracles; his Resurrection and Ascension; the coming of the Holy Spirit at Pentecost; and Jesus' second coming at the end of the world.

Without any one of these miracles, we would have a different religion. For instance, without Creation, we have the ancient heresy of Gnosticism. (The Gnostics thought that matter was the source of evil, so they denied that God created matter.) Without Resurrection, Christianity is a lie, says Saint Paul:

> We are shown to be lying about God, because we said that he raised Christ from death. . . . And if Christ has not been raised, then your faith is a delusion and you are

still lost in your sins. It would also mean that the believers in Christ who have died are lost. If our hope in Christ is good for this life only and no more, then we deserve more pity than anyone else in all the world (1 Cor 15:15–19).

Jesus' life was summed up by Saint Peter in Acts 10:38 in this way: "He went everywhere, doing good." But what good did he do? He did not run for political office; he did not found schools or hospitals; he did not fight a war to liberate the Jews from the Romans. Erase his miracles, and what good did he do?

Jesus himself appealed to the miracles he did as a reason to believe in him:

> When John the Baptist heard in prison about the things that Christ was doing, he sent some of his disciples to him. "Tell us," they asked Jesus, "Are you the one John said was going to come [the Messiah], or should we expect someone else?" Jesus answered, "Go back and tell John what you are hearing and seeing: the blind can see, the lame can walk, those who suffer from dreaded skin diseases are made clean, the deaf hear, the dead are brought back to life, and the Good News is preached to the poor" (Mt 11:2–5).

Jesus invited us to "Believe because of the [miraculous] things I do" (Jn 14:11).

The history of the Church is full of miracles, especially in the lives of the saints. Many of these miracles have been investigated with extreme care and scientific precision. The Church never canonizes a saint without proof of miracles worked through the saint's intercession. And the people who examine the supposed miracles have to include unbelievers, too. Thousands of carefully documented and proved miracles have taken place at Lourdes and Fatima, where the Blessed Virgin Mary appeared publicly. At Fatima 70,000 people witnessed the miracle of the sun dancing through the sky. There is a woman in Italy today who has no pupils in her eyes, yet she sees; she was healed by Padre Pio, who performed hundreds of miracles of healing. Anyone can see this continuous miracle, and many others, like the blood of Saint Januarius, hundreds of years old, turning liquid once every year, right out in public for anyone who is open-minded to see.

Open-minded investigators of miracles almost always are convinced. Only those who stubbornly hold onto their religious dogma that miracles cannot happen, continue to refuse to believe in miracles despite all the scientific evidence. It was the same in Jesus' day: if you simply *will* not believe, then even a miracle will not convince you. Read Jesus' story of the rich man and the poor man in Luke 16:19–31. Jesus warns there that people whose self-indulgent lifestyle would be threatened by religious faith "will not be convinced even if someone were to rise from death".

57. How do religion, science, and miracles fit together?

In the past, some Christians have sometimes opposed science because they were afraid that it somehow threatened their faith. This attitude is totally wrong. Some discoveries in some sciences have disproved some beliefs in some religions, yes. For instance, the discovery that lightning is caused by electrical storms disproved the ancient Greek belief that a god named Zeus manufactured lightning bolts and hurled them down to earth whenever he got angry. But *no* discovery of *any* science has *ever* disproved *any* of the doctrines of Christianity. Every new thing we learn by science about God's world is a new understanding of God's wisdom and a new reason to praise and love him. The psalmist says, "How clearly the sky reveals God's glory! How plainly it shows what he has done!" (Ps 19:1). Saint Paul says that God can be known through the world he created, "for God himself made it plain. Ever since God created the world, his invisible qualities, both his eternal power and his divine nature, have been clearly seen; they are perceived in the things that God has made" (Rom 1:19–20).

Of course, science can be misused. Anything can. But do not let yourself be intimidated by atheists who claim that science disproves God. That is like claiming that studying Shakespeare's plays disproves Shakespeare. If there were no God, there would be no science, because there would be no world for science to know.

Likewise, belief in science does not contradict belief in miracles. Science studies the way things usually work in the world, and it formulates laws to express these ways. Miracles are exceptions to these laws, but miracles presuppose these laws. If there were no scientific laws, there would be no sense in calling anything a miracle.

Exceptions to a law do not disprove the law. Suppose the President pardons a criminal. The laws of the court still hold, but the President adds something else from outside. The laws of the court are like the laws of science, and the Presidential pardon is like a miracle.

Suppose your employer gives you extra money for Christmas, over and above your paycheck. That does not disprove your contract, which tells you how much you usually get in your paycheck; it just adds to it. That is what a miracle does.

When an artist or musician creates his work of art, he usually obeys certain laws of art. But every once in a while he will make an exception. For instance, a novelist might not name his main character, or a painter might add some sand to his flat canvas, or a musician might add a new instrument to a symphony orchestra just for this one symphony. The artist does this for a good reason; it is not arbitrary. So does God. Each miracle he performs makes sense, teaches a lesson. In fact, the word for "miracle" in the New Testament means "sign" in Greek. A sign points to something. It is not arbitrary and irrational. It is meaningful.

If there is a God, there can be miracles. If there is no God, there can be no miracles, because there is no one who has the supernatural power to do them.

God created the world by intelligent design. That is why science is possible. It is no accident that science arose in the West, which believed in the doctrine of the Creation, not in the Orient, which did not. Most of the great scientists in history have been Jews, Christians, and Muslims, because these three religions believe that the world is created, therefore intelligently designed, ordered. Science and religion are allies, not enemies.

58. Does evolution contradict the Bible?

The Bible is primarily a book about God and humans. From it we learn who God is and who we are, we learn about God's love toward us and our actions toward him. In this sense, the Bible is a religious and moral book and not a textbook on scientific natural history. So we look to the Bible for God's message for the world he created, not for the scientific details about the process of creation.

The Book of Genesis presents these basic theological truths: the existence of God who created all things, the creation of the human race in the image and likeness of God, and the fact that God is not responsible for any of the evils found in the world. But Genesis doesn't teach exactly *how* God created.

Evolution teaches that lower forms of life went through a series of changes which eventually resulted in the development of human beings. Because it is a scientific theory, it could be proved or disproved in the future. But even if indisputable scientific proof of this theory is produced, the teaching of Genesis remains true: God created all things and created the human race in his own image and likeness.

The professional, scientific study of the anthropologist does not contradict the professional, religious work of the theologian as long as you remember two things: (1) The human *soul* is immediately created by God and does not evolve from a lower form of life; (2) all true human beings after Adam and Eve were generated from the first parents.

Theology and natural science are two distinct disciplines, each with its proper methods. We have to keep those distinctions in mind as we try to compare origins according to science and origins according to the Bible.

For further reading see *The Catholic Encyclopedia*, Nelson, 1976, pp. 202–3 and the *New Catholic Encyclopedia*, McGraw Hill, 1967, pp. 693–94. Two relevant encyclicals are *Divino Afflante Spiritu*, 1943, and *Humani Generis*, 1950, both written by Pope Pius XII.

59. Couldn't Jesus be just a good man?

That is the one thing he couldn't possibly be. A man who claims to be God is not a good man. He is either a bad man or he is God.

If he knows he is not God and still says he is and wants you to worship him, then he is a very bad man indeed: a liar and a blasphemer. If he thinks he is God but isn't, then he is insane. Jesus is either "Lord, liar, or lunatic."

But no one who reads the Gospels and gets to know the character of Jesus thinks he is a liar or a lunatic, a bad man or insane. Everyone admits he is a good man. Not only is he morally good, but he is also trustable. He is no fool, or wimp, or worm. He is incredibly wise. He sees into people's hearts (Mk 2:6–8).

But if he is wise, then you can trust what he says. And what he says is that he is God (Jn 5:17–18). That's why he was crucified (Jn 19:5–7). It was the only honest alternative to worshiping him. If he was not God, then he was the biggest liar and worst blasphemer in history.

When God revealed his own true name to Moses from the burning bush (Ex 3:14), it was the name "I Am." No one can say that name without claiming to *be* that person. It's not a name like "Joe" that you can say and mean someone else. When you say "I Am", you mean yourself. That's why no Jew ever pronounces that word. It would be blasphemy; it would be claiming to be God. And Jesus deliberately spoke that word, explicitly claimed to be God. Read John 8:48–59 for the most shocking thing that has ever been said by human lips.

Why then do people say Jesus was a good man but not God? Maybe because they refuse to follow him; they just want to be on their own. They want him to be at their beck and call, like a book on a shelf, a famous teacher they can study but not a living God who has claims on them.

For further reading on who Jesus is, read Matthew 18:18–20; John 1:1–2, 14–15; 2 Corinthians 5:21; Colossians 1:15–19, 2:8–10; 1 Timothy 2:5; Hebrews 1:8. Even the Old Testament writers anticipated who Jesus would be. Read Psalm 2:7 and Isaiah 53:11.

60. Did Jesus literally rise from the dead?

You will find some people, even some theologians, arguing that it does not matter. They say that we should not focus our attention on the physical resurrection of Jesus' dead body, because that is too crude, too gross, too physical. They say that the really important thing is the "spiritual meaning" of the Resurrection, the "resurrection of Easter faith" in the hearts of Jesus' disciples.

That idea is nonsense. Death is a crude, gross, and physical problem. It needs a crude, gross, and physical solution. You don't solve the problem of death by "resurrection of spiritual faith in the heart", but by a resurrection of the body.

The earliest creed, the "Apostles' Creed", includes as one of its twelve fundamental articles of belief "the resurrection of the body". The idea that when you die only your soul lives on is *not* a Christian idea. It comes from the pagan Greek philosophers.

God created us as a unity of body and soul (Gen 2:7). He warned Adam and Eve that the consequence of sin was physical death (Gen 2:17). Sin is the spiritual death of the soul; its separation from God, who is the source of its life. The spiritual death of the soul necessarily infects the body, too, because body and soul are one person. "Sin pays its wages—death" (Rom 6:23). Jesus solved both problems together. He solved the problem of sin, took the punishment for our sin, on the Cross. And he solved the problem of death when he rose from the dead. Only because he rose from death can we rise from death. That is the message of the New Testament, repeated many times. (See Jn 11:25–26 and Jn 14:19 for examples.)

If Jesus' Resurrection is only a myth, then Christianity is a lie. The apostles' teaching centered on the Resurrection. The "good news", or "gospel", that set the world on fire was not "you should love your neighbor." That's *good*, but it's not *news*. Christianity is "good news", the news that Jesus rose from the dead, proving his divinity and our salvation (1 Cor 15). The Church is essentially the community of witnesses to the Resurrection. The Church continues the work of the first apostles, to tell the world this "good news". *We* know it only because the Church has done its work for two thousand years.

There is very good logical reason to believe the Resurrection. If Jesus did not really rise from the dead, then the story is a lie. If it is not true, it is the most successful lie in history. Millions of people have based their lives on it. Who invented it? A lie, like a truth, must originate somewhere. It must have been Jesus' disciples, or the early Christian community. What was their motive for inventing and telling this lie? What did they get out of telling the lie?

I will tell you what they got out of it. Their friends and families hated and scorned them, thinking them crazy or wicked. Their social status, their political power, and their possessions were stolen from them. They were put in prison, whipped, beheaded, crucified, boiled in oil, fed to lions, hacked to pieces by gladiators in the Roman arena, sawed in pieces, and clubbed to death (Acts 5:38–40, 7:54–60, 8:1–3). If the miracle of the Resurrection did not really happen, then an even more incredible miracle happened: twelve Jewish men invented an incredible myth for no reason at all and died for it, and so did millions of others. This "lie" transformed lives, softened hardened criminals, hardened soft-hearted cowards, gave cynics hope and joy, gave people in despair a reason to live and a reason to die, and put hymns on the lips of martyrs—all for no reason at all, for a fantastic practical joke, a myth. Yes, that story is fantastic indeed. *That* story is the myth, not Christianity.

61. How can I know there is life after death?

Jesus assures us that there is, and proves it by rising from the dead himself, *showing* us the Resurrection.

If there is no life after death, then God is either weak or unloving: either too weak to conquer death for us, or too unloving to care about us enough to give us life.

If there is no life after death, then the teachings of Jesus are a lie, for he constantly talked about life after death, "The kingdom of Heaven", Heaven and Hell.

If there is no life after death, then life is a cruel joke.

If there is no life after death, then we are only smart animals, with bodies and brains but no souls.

If there is no life after death, then we have no hope of ever seeing God face-to-face, ever attaining complete joy, and ever seeing our dead loved ones again.

If there is no life after death, then life before death is cheap, like a pregnancy that will not survive. If a pregnant woman hopes that her baby will be born alive, she takes care of it. But if she thinks it will be born dead, she no longer thinks of it as very precious. This life is like being in the womb, and death is like being born.

"But the truth is that Christ has been raised from death, as the guarantee that those who sleep in death will also be raised" (1 Cor 15:20). Read that whole great chapter sometime, 1 Corinthians 15. It concludes with this difference that life after death makes: "You know that nothing you do in the Lord's service is ever useless" (1 Cor 15:58).

The writer of Ecclesiastes, a philosophical book in the Old Testament, did not believe in life after death. (See Eccl 3:19–22.) The result of this belief was that he saw life as "vanity of vanities, all is vanity" (Eccl 1:2). Read that whole pessimistic book sometime to see the difference life after death makes. A second author answered him in the last two verses (Eccl 12:13–14), which say that because we will be judged by God after death, therefore life has meaning: "Have reverence for God and obey his commands, because this is all that man was created for." We will meet him one day. We must not turn away from that wonderful and awesome truth, or our lives will become cheap and meaningless.

62. What is Heaven like?

Imagine the very best Heaven you can. Then go beyond that to infinity.

"What no eye has seen, nor ear heard, nor the heart of man conceived, what God has prepared for those who love him" (1 Cor 2:9).

The essence of Heaven is the presence of God, the source of all joy and love. Every little bit of joy we ever experience on earth is like a sunbeam from the sun of God. In Heaven we will experience joy at its source.

Perhaps you think you'll be bored in Heaven because you're thinking of popular pictures of fluffy white clouds and angels playing harps. That is not the Bible's picture of Heaven. No one will be bored in Heaven. If you are bored with church services, don't be afraid; there are no church services in Heaven. John, who had a vision of Heaven and wrote it down in the Book of Revelation, said, "I did not see a temple in the [Heavenly] city, because its temple is the Lord God Almighty and the Lamb" (Rev 21:22).

The language of the Bible about Heaven is full of poetic symbols, because Heaven is so much more wonderful than earth that earthly language can't express it literally, any more than words can express music, or colors can be explained to blind people. Revelation 21 and 22 describe the New Jerusalem as a city shining like a precious stone, clear as crystal. Its wall is made of jasper and its foundations are adorned with precious stones. Its twelve gates are made of pearl and its streets of pure gold. The glory of God lights this city, and nothing impure is found in it. The river of the water of life flows from the throne of God, and on each side of the river is a tree of life, the leaves of which are for the healing of the nations. Whatever Heaven is, it is God's plan for us, and God is very wise, very good, very loving, and very full of surprises.

63. Is there really a Hell?

Jesus said there was. Who is more of an authority on the subject than he is? Jesus talked more about Hell than anyone in the Bible—not because he enjoyed scaring people but because He loved them and wanted to save them from it. When there are holes in the ice, the loving thing to do is to put up clear warning signs. That's what the Bible does. Only a fool ignores God's warning signs just because other fools in society ignore them.

Jesus described Hell as "fire" (Mk 9:47–48). (It is not earthly fire, any more than Hell is an earthly place. You can't put the fire of Hell out with a fire hose any more than you can get to Hell in a fire truck.) Fire *destroys* things. Hell is where what once was a human being, an individual soul, a real person, is destroyed. Hell is far worse than the popular picture of a torture chamber. In a torture chamber, you lose only your peace, your pleasure, your health. In Hell, you lose your very self, your soul.

In Hell you lose God. God is not one among many sources of joy, happiness, light, life, and meaning for our lives. He is the only source of all of it, for he alone created everything that is good. To lose God is to lose *everything*. Hell is life's only final tragedy. Jesus saves us from that tragedy. Not to accept his gift of salvation is the stupidest thing anyone can possibly do. And the last.

Jesus is the Noah's ark that protects us from the flood of Hell. Jesus is the blood of the Passover lamb that protects us from the angel of death (Ex 12). Jesus is the "life-giving water" (Jn 4:10–14, 7:37–39) that quenches the fires of Hell. The very name *Jesus* means "Savior". That is his task. That is why he came to earth to die: to save us from sin and death and Hell. That may sound old-fashioned, but it is the heart of Christianity, of Jesus' own teaching. If there is nothing eternal for Jesus to save us *from*, then he is not our eternal *Savior*.

64. What does God want most?

This question has already been asked—in the Bible. And the same answer given almost 2,000 years ago is true today. Here is what Saint Mark recorded:

> A teacher of the Law was there who heard the discussion. He saw that Jesus had given the Sadducees a good answer, so he came to him with a question: "Which commandment is the most important of all?"
>
> Jesus replied, "The most important one is this: 'Listen, Israel! The Lord our God is the only Lord. Love the Lord your God with all your heart, with all your soul, with all

your mind, and with all your strength.' The second most important commandment is this: 'Love your neighbor as you love yourself.' There is no other commandment more important than these two."

The teacher of the Law said to Jesus, "Well done, Teacher! It is true, as you say, that only the Lord is God and that there is no other god but he. And man must love God with all his heart and with all his mind and with all his strength; and he must love his neighbor as he loves himself. It is more important to obey these two commandments than to offer on the altar animals and other sacrifices to God."

Jesus noticed how wise his answer was, and so he told him, "You are not far from the Kingdom of God" (Mk 12:28–34).

Once we know the answer to the question "What does God want most?" we also know the answer to the question "What is the meaning of life?" That is the most important of all questions. The simple answer to Question One of the old classic Baltimore Catechism summarizes the whole Bible's answer: "To know, love, and serve God in this life and enjoy him forever in the next." *That* is what God wants most from us.